Maritime Law
Volume II Enforced Sales of Vessels

INTERNATIONAL BAR ASSOCIATION

Maritime Law
Volume II Enforced Sales of Vessels

Edited by

LENNART HAGBERG

Written by
Members of the Committee on Maritime and Transport Law
of the Section on Business Law
of the International Bar Association

1977
Springer-Science+Business Media, B.V.

ISBN 978-94-017-4376-1 ISBN 978-94-017-4374-7 (eBook)
DOI 10.1007/978-94-017-4374-7

Cover design: Pieter J. van der Sman

Originally published by Kluwer B.V., Deventer/The Netherlands in 1977.
Softcover reprint of the hardcover 1st edition 1977

Table of Contents

List of Contributors

Editor:

Lennart Hagberg, advokat, Mannheimer & Zetterlöf KB, Gothenburg

Contributors:

Australia
by John de Koning, solicitor, Ellison Hewison & Whitehead, Melbourne

Belgium
by Tony Kegels, advocat, Antwerpen

Canada
by John R. Cunningham, barrister and solicitor, Macrae, Montgomery, Spring & Cunningham, Vancouver

Denmark
by Jan Erlund, advokat, Copenhagen

Finland
by Henrik Langenskiöld, advokat, Serlachius & Ryti, Helsinki

France
by Jacques Villeneau, avocat à la Cour, Paris

Germany
by Dr. H.-Chr. Albrecht, Hasche, Albrecht, Fischer, Hamburg

Greece
by P. C. Panagopoulos of the Athens Bar, Athens

Ireland
by G. John Moloney, solicitor, Jermyn & Moloney, Cork

Italy
by Attilio Costabel, avvocato, Genoa

Japan
by Yoichi Ogawa, captain, counsellor at law, Tokyo

Malta
by R. Farrugia, solicitor, Birkirkara

The Netherlands
by Dr. F. Baron van der Feltz, advocat, Loeff, van der Feltz & Salomonson, Amsterdam

Norway
by Alex. Rein, høyesterettsadvokat, Wikborg, Rein, Ringdal & Waelgaard, Oslo

Singapore
by T. H. A. Potts, advocate and solicitor, Rodyk & Davidson, Singapore

South Africa
by The Maritime Law Association of the Republic of South Africa, Cape Town

Spain
by Ignacio Arroyo, professor of Mercantile Law, LL.M. Harvard, University Autonoma of Madrid

Sweden
by Robert Romlöv, advokat, Vinge & Ramberg Advokatbyrå, Gothenburg

United Kingdom
by J. G. R. Griggs, solicitor, Ince and Co., St. Helier, Jersey, Channel Islands

United States of America
by John C. McHose, attorney, Lillick, McHose, Wheat, Adams & Charles, Los Angeles

Foreword

It gives me great pleasure as Chairman of the Section on Business Law to write a foreword to this, the second volume in a series of books on Maritime Law. Volume I dealt with 'Arrest of Vessels' and the remaining subjects to be covered are 'Mortgages of Vessels' and 'Registration of Vessels'. The first volume has proved most successful and many lawyers have testified to its practical value. I am certain that this second volume will have an equally warm welcome.

The series is the inspiration of Lennart Hagberg, the Chairman of the Section on Business Law's Committee on Maritime and Transport Law. Both he, and the contributors to the series who are all members of that Committee, are busy practising lawyers, and it is only by making sacrifices that they have been able to add this additional task to their already heavy commitments. In particular, Lennart Hagberg's task as editor has involved an enormous amount of work and I am most grateful to him and his fellow-contributors for all that they have done.

May I wish this Book and those following it every success.

JACQUES LASSIER

Chairman

Paris 1977

Editor's Note

The second part of the handbook on maritime law under production by the Maritime and Transport Law Committee of the Section of Business Law of the International Bar Association is now being published through the kind offices of Kluwer B. V., Deventer, The Netherlands. This part deals with the requirements for an enforced sale of a vessel.

The same system has been used in preparing the second part as for the first part. A questionnaire was sent out. On the basis of the answers received I prepared a draft for each country which was sent to the respective contributors for revision and approval. To the largest extent possible uniform headlines have been used.

The purpose of the handbook is to assist the practising lawyer to get an overall view which will prepare him for the requirements of the colleague he will consult or instruct in a foreign country where a vessel is or is contemplated to be sold.

It has not been our intention to prepare a full treatise in comparative law or even to cover all practical questions which may arise in connection with an enforced sale.

I have to add the same note of caution as I did in my note to Part I. The handbook is not intended and should not be used as a basis for a 'do it yourself job'. A local lawyer should be consulted.

The Section of Business Law, the editor or the contributors do not assume any responsibility for the accuracy of the contents of the various articles.

I should like to express my thanks to the individual contributors for their renewed efforts, to the Director-General of the International Bar Association, Sir Thomas Lund, and to his staff for their encouragement and assistance. In particular I would also like to thank Mr. J. G. R. Griggs of Jersey who has taken the trouble to read and revise most of the text.

I am also glad to mention that I understand from our publishers that Part I of our handbook has turned out to be a success and I do hope that Part II will follow this example.

I would also like to mention that Parts III and IV on Registration and Mortgages on Ships respectively will now be prepared.

February 1977

Editor's Introduction

As indicated in my note I have tried to use uniform headlines to the greatest extent possible in order to assist the reader. I will now briefly set out the subjects intended to be covered under those headlines.

Grounds for an enforced Sale

It is of utmost importance to know the requirements necessary to request an enforced sale. Generally speaking in most countries a judgment is necessary but in good many countries in addition Mortgagees have special rights.

Authority

Country by country a description of the authorities handling an enforced sale is found under this headline.

Care and Maintenance of the Vessel pending Sale

It is essential to know whether the authorities in charge of the sale will take care of the vessel or the Claimant himself must take action. In some countries a third type of solution is found. The authorities take care of the vessel but the Claimant must advance the monies. The answers to those questions are found under this headline.

Appraisal

Under this headline are found particulars country by country whether the authority in charge of the sale arranges for an official appraisal of the vessel or not.

Notice of Sale

A notice of sale has two main functions. The first one is to bring the sale to the knowledge of a shipping community in a manner to interest as wide a selection of prospective buyers as possible in order to obtain a good price in the common interest of the Creditors.

The second purpose is to notify the individual Creditor of the sale in order to enable the Creditor to protect his interests. In particular it is of special interest for the Mortgagees to know whether they as registered Mortgagees are automatically notified by the relevant authority of the intended sale. The answers to such questions should be found here.

Form of actual Sale

Answers to the questions whether a vessel is sold by private treaty or at a public auction are found under this headline. It is of interest to the Creditors to know whether the Creditors themselves are able to buy the vessel in order to protect their interests.

Minimum Price or any Price

For all the Creditors, in particular the Mortgagees, it is of interest to know whether there are special rules so far as the price is concerned in order to protect the Creditors. The answers to those questions are found here.

Payment of Price

Particularly for a Creditor who in order to protect his interests is prepared to bid for the vessel himself it is necessary to know whether the price must be paid in full in cash or credit terms are available. The system for payment is described country by country under this headline.

Distribution of the Proceeds

For a Creditor it is of course important to know in which way he must file and prove his claim and in which way he can obtain payment.

A description country by country of the legal machinery available is found under this headline. It may be added that in all countries the distribution of the proceeds is in the hands of official authorities although of course the rules in detail vary country by country.

Appeal Proceedings

For a Creditor it is important to know what sort of legal remedies are at his disposal should he not be satisfied with the actions taken or decisions made by the authorities in charge of an enforced sale. The possibilities of an appeal or similar proceedings are explained country by country under this headline.

International Conventions

An international convention for the unification of certain rules of law relating to maritime liens and mortgages was concluded in Brussels in 1967. This Convention gives detailed rules in respect of international recognition of mortgages on ships, of maritime liens, priorities etc. One of the basic principles of that Convention is that the states bound by the Convention must mutually recognise and respect mortgages and maritime liens created in such a state. For that reason it is important to know whether the country in question is a party to that Convention or not. The answers to this specific question are found under this headline.

About the International Bar Association

The IBA, primarily an Association of Bar Associations and Law Societies, was founded in 1947. It is non-political and its objects are:

> 'To establish and maintain permanent relations and exchanges between Bar Associations thoughout the world and their members.'
> 'To discuss problems of professional organisation and status.'
> 'To assist Members of the legal profession throughout the world, whether in the field of legal education or otherwise, to develop and improve their legal services to the public. To advance the science of jurisprudence in all its phases. By common study of practical legal problems to promote uniformity and definition in appropriate fields of law.'
> 'To promote the administration of justice under law among the peoples of the world.'
> 'In execution of these objects, to promote in their legal aspects the principles and aims of the United Nations and to co-operate with and promote co-ordination among, international juridical organisations having similar purposes.'

It seeks generally to:

1. ensure better co-operation between and improvement in the services of all Bar Associations and Law Societies;
2. provide opportunities for individual lawyers to make personal contacts and by sharing their expertise to contribute towards the solution of common international legal problems; and
3. enable the voice of the legal profession to be heard on the international scene and so to contribute towards the establishment and maintenance of the Rule of Law throughout the world.

The IBA has consultative status with the United Nations Organisation and the Council of Europe and has Standing Committees on United Nations Affairs and European Affairs.

It organises annually Conferences and seminars and publishes the International Bar Journal biannually and the International Business Lawyer quarterly. It also publishes Directories of its Members.

There are two sections of the IBA, the Section on Business Law set up to promote an interchange of information among Members as to laws, practices and procedures affecting business, financial and commercial activities throughout the world and the Section on General Practice whose members are engaged in the general practice of law. The Section on Business Law has 20 Committees and the Section on General Practice 15 which work mainly by mail but meet at least annually and more frequently if the Chairman is satisfied that there is a need for it. Most Committees are engaged in the study of specific subjects within the field of their activities.

78 Bar Associations and Law Societies belong to the IBA as well as approaching 4000 individual lawyers. Further details of the Association and how to join may be obtained from the IBA, Byron House, 7–9 St. James's Street, London SW1A 1EE, England.

J. P. M. de Koning

Australia

Grounds for an enforced Sale

a. A judgment or order from the appropriate Supreme Court or from the High Court is necessary for the enforced sale of a vessel in civil proceedings.

b. Certain other public authorities have power to seize and sell vessels; e.g.

(i) The sale of any wreck whether claimed or unclaimed by the receiver of wreck in the exercise of powers granted him by Part VII of the Commonwealth Navigation Act 1912–1973;

(ii) The sale by a port officer or harbour master in the State of Victoria by order of any two Justices of the Peace in the exercise of powers granted under Section 13 of the Marine Act 1958 of the State of Victoria of any ship or boat sunk, stranded or run on shore in any port in Victoria;

(iii) The sale of vessels seized because of contravention by them or their owners of the provisions of the Commonwealth Fisheries Act 1952–1975 and their subsequent forfeiture to the Crown by the appropriate Magistrates Court;

(iv) The sale by a Minister of the Commonwealth of any ship wrecked, stranded, sunk or abandoned on or near the coast of Australia in the exercise of powers granted him by Part VII of the Commonwealth Navigation Act 1912–1973;

(v) In any case in which any Court directs payment of any sum of money by any party, being the master or owner of a ship, and that party does not pay it in accordance with the Order, the Court making the Order may, in addition to any of its other powers, direct the amount or the portion thereof remaining unpaid to be levied by distress and sale of the whole or any portion of the ship and her equipment, and they shall be sold accordingly. Section 399 Commonwealth Navigation Act 1912–1973.

c. (i) The general rule in Australia seems to be that attempts by owners or others interested in the vessel (e.g. mortgagees) to sell a vessel privately when she is subject to an Order for sale by a Court will be treated as contempt. *The Ruth Kayser* (1925) 23 LlLR 95, although the Court appears to have inherent power to grant approval to a mortgagee for a private sale subject to appropriate terms – *The Monmouth Court* (1922) 12 LlLR 22;

(ii) A first mortgagee in possession is entitled to complete control over the ship and thus has absolute power to dispose of her or the share in respect of which he is registered. A subsequent mortgagee may not however do so except under order of a Court of competent jurisdiction or by prior consent of the earlier mortgagees. The sale may be privately or by public auction but the mortgagee in exercising his power of sale must act bona-fide and must not recklessly disregard the rights of the mortgagor. He must take reasonable steps to obtain a fair price – *Pendlebury* v. *Colonial Mutual Life* (1911) 13 CLR 676.

Authority

The Marshal of the High Court and the Sheriff of the Supreme Court are the authorities who handle the sale in any civil proceedings involving an action In Rem. In the case of sale following criminal or quasi-criminal proceedings the person appointed by the relevant Act is the authorised person to handle the sale.

Care and Maintenance of the Vessel pending Sale

The Marshal or the Sheriff in civil actions as the case may be, having arrested the vessel and thus having taken custody of it, is responsible for its safe preservation while awaiting sale. These persons are secured for their expenses by the persons who caused the vessel to be arrested, although once the vessel is sold such expenses are usually paid out of the proceeds. In other proceedings the relevant authority may be under a duty to preserve the vessel.

Appraisal

The rules of both the High Court and the Supreme Court provide for the possibility of appraisement before the sale of the vessel. The relevant rules are –

a. High Court Rules Order 50 Rules 2, 4, 10, 11 and 12 –

'2. A sale, mortgage, partition or exchange ordered by the Court or a Justice shall be carried out in accordance with directions given by a Justice in Chambers;

4. (1) Where a judgment or order is given or made, whether in Court or in Chambers, directing any property to be sold, unless otherwise ordered the property shall be sold by auction, with the approbation of the Justice, to the best purchaser that can be got for it, to be approved by the Justice.

(2) All proper parties shall join in the sale and conveyance or transfer as the Justice directs.

10. (1) A commission for the appraisement or sale of property under the order of the Court shall, unless the Court or a Justice otherwise orders, be executed by the Marshal or his Deputies or officers.

(2) A solicitor who takes out a commission for appraisement or sale shall file an undertaking to pay the fees and expenses of the Marshal or his Deputy if they are demanded.

11. (1) The Marshal or his Deputy shall pay into Court the gross proceeds of any property which has been sold by him.

(2) The Marshal or his Deputy shall bring into Court the account for sale, with vouchers in support of the account, for taxation by the Registrar of the Registry in which the proceeding is pending.

12. (1) A person interested in the proceeds may be heard before the Registrar on the taxation of the Marshal's or Deputy Marshal's account of expenses.

(2) An objection to the taxation shall be heard in the same manner as an objection to the taxation of a solicitor's bill of costs.'

b. Supreme Court Admiralty Rules 70–79 –

'70. The Court or a Judge may, either before or after final judgment, order any property under the arrest of the Court to be appraised, or to be sold with or without appraisement, and either by public auction or by private contract.

71. If the property is deteriorating in value, the Court or a Judge may order it to be sold forthwith.

72. If the property to be sold is of small value, the Court or a Judge may order it to be sold without a commission of sale being issued.

73. The Court or a Judge may, either before or after final judgment, order any property under arrest of the Court to be removed, or any cargo under arrest on board ship to be discharged.
74. The appraisement, sale and removal of property, the discharge of cargo, and the demolition and sale of a ship condemned under any Slave Trade Act, shall, except as provided by Rules 71 and 72 be effected under the authority of a commission addressed to the Sheriff and executed by the Sheriff.
75. The commission shall, as soon as possible after its execution, be filed by the Sheriff with a return setting forth the manner in which it has been executed.
76. As soon as possible after the execution of a commission of sale the Sheriff shall pay into Court the gross proceeds of the sale, and shall with the commission file his accounts and vouchers in support thereof.
77. The Prothonotary shall tax the Sheriff's account and shall certify the amount at which he considers it should be allowed and any party who is interested in the proceeds may be heard before the Prothonotary on the taxation.
78. Application may be made to the Court or a Judge on motion to review the Prothonotary's taxation.
79. The Court or a Judge may order any property under the arrest of the Court to be inspected.'

Notice of Sale

a. The practice stated in McGuffie, Fugeman and Gray, Volume 1 of British Shipping Laws, *Admiralty Practice*, paragraph 387, page 170 –

'The usual order for sale made by the court directs that the Marshal shall sell by public auction or private treaty. Sales today are almost always by private treaty but in every case the expert advice of the Marshal's broker as to the best method of sale is obtained'

is generally applied by both the High Court and the Supreme Court.

In this context 'private treaty' involves advertisement in various newspapers, without an asking price, sealed offers to be sent in before a fixed time on a fixed date.

As appears from Rules 71 and 72 of the Supreme Court quoted above this practice is not followed in every instance, other more appropriate procedures being permitted.

b. Because of the rule requiring maintenance of priorities it is normal for all known creditors to be advised of the sale although this is not an absolute requirement.

c. It is usual practice for notice of the enforced sale to be sent to the registered owner of the vessel.

d. Although it is not a requirement for the enforced sale that particulars be obtained from the Register of the vessel as to title to the vessel, mortgages and other encumbrances, in order to maintain priorities such particulars are obtained wherever possible.

Form of actual Sale

The vessel is sold by the Marshal of the High Court, the Sheriff of the Supreme Court or other relevant authority appointed for that purpose.

See also above under Notice of Sale, *a.*

Minimum Price or any Price

Upon a commission of appraisement and sale having been issued the Marshal or Sheriff as the case may be must employ an appraiser to make an inventory of the vessel and her equipment which may not be sold below the appraised value (Form 21 Admiralty rules, Supreme Court).

Because of the mode of sale adopted there is nothing to prevent creditors from purchasing the vessel themselves in order to protect their own interests.

Payment of Price

a. Because of the form of the Rules of Court and the form of the Commission of Sale issued under them payment is required in cash, and within the time ordered;

b. Payment is to be made to the Marshal or Sheriff as the case may be who must pay into Court the gross proceeds of the sale.

Distribution of the Proceeds

a. Since distribution of the proceeds of sale can only proceed by order of the Court (High Court Order 23 Rule 8 (1), Supreme Court Rule 95) any person claiming an interest in the fund in Court is entitled to be heard (High Court Order 50 Rule 12 (1), Supreme Court Rule 77).

Alternatively each creditor could proceed to judgment in an action begun in his name preventing any payment out of court by filing a caveat (High Court Order 30 Rule 20, Supreme Court Rule 87).

b. In Australia claims against the fund are ranked in order of priority, these are usually ranked as follows –

First: Statutory Liens e.g. Marshal's or Sheriff's charges;
Second: Plaintiff's costs;
Third: Maritime Liens;
Fourth: Possessory Liens;
Fifth: Mortgages;
Sixth: Maritime claims entitling a claimant to arrest the vessel e.g. supply of necessaries.

A full summary of the priorities is contained in British Shipping Laws, Vol. 1, *Admiralty Practice,* supra, paragraph 1574, pages 742–746.

c. Where foreign vessels are concerned the lex fori is applied.

d. It is generally considered possible for creditors by unanimous agreement as to distribution of the proceeds of sale to decide on such distribution subject to Court approval of such agreement.

Appeal Proceedings

The normal rules of appeal apply with respect to any finding as to priority among creditors or from any order or judgment of a Court relating to the sale of a vessel.

International Conventions

Australia has not become a party to the Convention for the Unification of Certain Rules of Law relating to Maritime Liens and Mortgages 1967.

Other points of interest

Following the decision of the High Court in *Shell Oil Co. Ltd.* v. *The Ship 'Lastrigoni'* (1974) 48 ALJR 295 it may well be that in Australia the right to arrest a ship and thus to sell it is more limited than previously accepted. It was there ruled that it is only possible to arrest a vessel in respect of maritime claims secured by maritime liens provided that at the time of the bringing of the action a right in personam is also available against the owner of the vessel. This limitation is open to doubt as a matter of principle.

Tony Kegels

Belgium

Grounds for an enforced Sale

In principle there is no difference between the civil and commercial law and the maritime law relating the grounds for an enforced sale: Belgian law requires a 'title', that is to say an official document proving the existence of the claim.

Such a title for the enforcement of a sale can be either a final judgment of a Court or an authentic act of a public notary, e.g. for a mortgage upon a ship.

Judgments of foreign Courts and a notarial Act of a foreign notary can also be the basis for an enforced sale, provided they are enforceable in Belgium (exequatur).

A private request or a private title are not sufficient to enforce the sale of a ship – only a public title is admissible.

Authority

The sale of a ship is subject to a rather complicated official procedure as explained in articles 1545 to 1559 of the Procedure Law and some other general articles relating enforced sale in general.

In a few words one may summarise as follows:

Providing there is a public title one can enforce the sale subject to a number of different official notifications, the appointment of the auctioneer by a specialised Judge, who controls also the distribution of the proceeds of the sale. As a matter of fact, one may say that a public sale is entirely under the control of the Judge. For details see further.

Care and maintenance of the Vessel pending Sale

The law does not place upon the party who asks for a sale an obligation to preserve the ship. This duty is still that of the owner but, mostly, the bailiffs arrange for watchmen to be put on board and to stay there. The costs of such 'gardienna' are considered as official privileged costs with a priority claim against the proceeds.

Appraisal

No official valuation is made prior to the sale of the ship.

Notice of Sale

The law requires a number of notices in Art. 1499 to 1528. A first notification must be served the day before the arrest of the ship and this notification must contain the title (see above) of the creditor, the Judge who eventually will intervene, the amount claimed and all details of the ship, tonnage etc.

This notification is served upon the debtor or, if it is a maritime claim, possibly upon the captain or an officer. If the ship does not belong to the debtor, this notification must also be served upon the owner of the ship or his agent, if in the port.

Once this first notification is served one may arrest the ship and such an arrest is valid for one year. This arrest is notified to the captain, and within three days to the owner and to the debtor and is also notified to the ship's registry, even if it concerns a foreign vessel.

The next step is the request to the Judge for the appointment of a public auctioneer to sell the ship. The Judge makes an order specifying a requirement for advertising the sale and nominating the place of sale.

This order is not served and remains in fact a matter of procedure.

Once the auctioneer is appointed, he has to draft the conditions of the sale, mentioning the exact place, hour and date of the auction.

Fifteen days before the sale this auctioneer must notify by bailiff to the debtor (owner of the ship) the conditions of the sale and this notification must also be given to the other creditors who are known to the auctioneer (by registered mail). Unfortunately Belgian law does not require the notification of the sale to the register of foreign vessels but, in practice this is often done.

It is a requirement that particulars of foreign mortgages and other registered encumbrances shall be obtained before the sale.

Form of actual Sale

The sale is actually conducted by the official auctioneer, appointed by the Court. This can be a bailiff, a notary or even a shipbroker.

Minimum Price or any Price

A ship can be sold at any price but can also be withdrawn if the price seems to be too low.

Creditors can attend, can buy the vessel and are allowed to protect their interests at any stage. They can i.a. interfere before the sale, ask for the intervention of the Judge if they consider that the sale conditions are badly drafted, etc. – this is the reason why the different notifications include the place of sale and the Judge to be approached.

Payment of Price

The price may be paid in cash but credit terms can be arranged with the public auctioneer. Normally he will ask for guarantees. Once the price is paid the funds are deposited in an official 'consignation' bank, the so-called 'Caisse de Dépôt de Consignation'. Then follows the next procedure, the distribution of the proceeds of the sale between the creditors.

Distribution of the Proceeds

Any creditor may intervene in the division of the proceeds until the moment they are distributed. Belgium applies the following priorities:

a. Maritime liens
b. Maritime mortgages
c. Liens under general law

The maritime liens are those provided for in the International Convention on Unification of Certain Rules of Law relating to Maritime Liens and Mortgages signed at Brussels, 10th April, 1926, summarised as follows:

1. Law costs due to the state, and expenses incurred in the common interest of the creditors in order to preserve the vessel or to procure its sale and the distribution of the proceeds of sale; tonnage dues, light and harbour dues, and other public taxes and charges of the

same character; pilotage dues; the costs of watching and preserving of the vessel;

2. Claims arising out of the contract of engagement of the master, crew and other persons hired on board;
3. Remuneration for assistance and salvage and the contribution on the vessel in general average;
4. Indemnities for collision or other accident of navigation, and also for damage caused to works forming part of harbours, docks, and navigable ways; indemnities for personal injury to passengers or crew; indemnities for loss of or damage to cargo or baggage;
5. Claims resulting from contracts entered into or acts done by the master, acting within the scope of his authority, away from the vessel's home port, where such contracts or acts are necessary for the preservation of the vessel or the continuation of its voyage, whether the master is or is not at the same time owner of the vessel, and whether the claim is his own or that of ship-chandlers, repairers, lenders, or other contractual creditors.

First these claims are paid, then the mortgagees on the vessels are paid and then possible claims, privileged under common law and, finally, the non-preferred creditors.

It has been a matter of dispute whether priority falls to be determined by the lex fori, by the law of the flag or by the law of the place where the claim arose. Although the Belgian authors were of opinion that the law of the flag should determine the priority rules, the Belgian Courts have decided that it is the lex fori (Court of Appeal Brussels 9/7/1939 – BA 1941 – P. 5; idem 12/5/1956 – BA 57 195) (Court of Brugge 8/5/1940 – BA 1940 357) (Court of Antwerp 1/6/1962 – BA 1962 368).

The creditors may agree upon the distribution of the proceeds but they have to pass their agreement through the adjuster (always an attorney), instructed by the Court.

Appeal Proceedings

The procedure on appeal is very complicated and we may say that practically at any stage of the procedure an appeal or opposition (if the decision was given by default) is possible.

As a principle of Belgian law one may consider that any decision, given unilaterally on request by a Judge or given by default by a Court is subject to the so called opposition. The delays are normally one month.

Further, any contradictory judgment (resulting out of proceedings where both parties were present) may be submitted to an appeal – delay also one month from the notification of the judgment.

Apart from these general rules one must keep in mind that an intervention of the Judge is always possible if difficulties arise during execution proceedings.

As far as distribution of the funds is concerned, normal legal procedure is followed, i.e. distribution is made after Court hearings, unless there is an appeal by a party disagreeing with the first decision.

International Conventions

Belgium adhered to the Convention of 10th April, 1926, in respect of maritime liens and mortgages, but not yet to the Convention for the unification of certain rules relating to maritime liens and mortgages of 27th May, 1967, which will replace and abrogate the former convention.

Belgium was a signatory to the international Convention relating to registration of rights in respect of vessels under construction (Brussels, 27th May, 1967) under reserve of approval and ratification but has not yet ratified this Convention.

I have to add that Belgium has anticipated this Convention, because the Belgian law (Art. 26 of 22/11/28) makes it possible to take a mortgage on a ship under construction.

John R. Cunningham

Canada

Grounds for an enforced Sale

a. A judgment or order from the Federal Court of Canada is necessary for an enforced sale of a vessel in civil proceedings.

b. There are provisions for a vessel being sold by other public authorities, examples of which are:

(i) The sale of an unclaimed wreck, by a receiver of wrecks, a person appointed by the Federal Government;

(ii) In any case in which a conviction has been secured against the owner of a ship for a contravention of any of the provisions of the Canada Shipping Act, and the fine is not paid, the ship may be sold by any chief officer of customs, or other person authorised by the Minister of Transport.

c. A vessel can be sold at an enforced sale on the basis of 'a private request' if the request is made by a person holding a first mortgage against the vessel (or by a subsequent mortgagee with the concurrence of every prior mortgagee). The mortgagee of a registered Canadian vessel has an absolute power of sale and can sell the vessel privately without a public auction and without Court proceedings. He is, however, required by law to take reasonable steps and precautions to obtain a proper price for the vessel, having regard to all the circumstances. If he does not, he stands the risk of being found liable to the owner for the difference between what the vessel sold for and a reasonably obtainable price. (see *Gulf & Fraser Fishermen's Credit Union* v. *Calm C. Fish Ltd. et al., The 'CALM C'* (1975) Lloyd's Law Reports 188).

Authority

The Federal Court of Canada is the authority that handles the sale in any civil proceeding involving an action in rem. In the case of a sale by a mortgagee of a Canadian vessel, the mortgagee can handle the sale himself or appoint a bailiff or agent to do it for him.

Care and Maintenance of the Vessel pending Sale

The Admiralty Marshal, upon the application of any interested party, by Court Order, and after having been secured for his fees and expenses, may take possession of the vessel arrested, and is responsible for her safe preservation while awaiting sale. Such fees and expenses are normally paid out of the proceeds from the sale.

Appraisal

A common practice is for an appraisal of the vessel to be carried out. This is not done in every instance and is not required by law, although it may be advisable to indicate prudence in cases where a vessel is not sold by a Court Order. The Federal Court rules provide that the vessel may be sold with or without appraisal, either by public auction or private contract.

Notice of Sale

a. A public notice is normally required prior to a sale by the Court and the proposed sale advertised in appropriate newspapers likely to be read by prospective buyers. However, the Federal Court Rules provide that the Court may direct what notice of the sale by advertisement or otherwise shall be given, or may dispense with notice. The extent of the notice given and the time between the publication of such a notice and the sale is usually decided by the Court upon application of the person who had the vessel arrested. Other interested parties are also entitled to make submissions with respect to where the sale should be advertised and how much time should be allowed before the sale. There is no minimum time between the publication of the notice and the sale.
b. It is the normal practice to notify mortgagees and other known creditors but it is not an absolute requirement.
c. It is normal practice for notice of the enforced sale to be sent to the registered owner of the vessel.

It is normal practice to obtain particulars from the register of the vessel as to title of the vessel and what mortgages and other registered encumbrances are on the vessel, but such particulars are not a requirement with respect to the right to an enforced sale.

Authority which performs the actual Sale

The actual sale by the Court is performed by the Admiralty Marshal, acting under the authority of a commission issued by the Court.

Minimum Price or any Price

A minimum price is often fixed by order of the Court, below which the vessel is not to be sold, after submissions have been made by the person who had the vessel arrested and other interested parties. It is not mandatory that a minimum price be fixed. After receiving offers to purchase the vessel, the Court may, after hearing the interested parties, if it is doubtful that a fair price has been offered, order that the amount of the highest offer be communicated to the other persons who made offers or to other persons, or otherwise take steps with a view to obtaining a higher offer.

Presence of Creditors

It is possible for creditors to be present and if necessary protect their interests by buying the vessel themselves.

Payment of Price

a. It is normal that the price be paid in cash, or within a stated time after the sale.
b. The payment for the vessel is made into Court.

Distribution of the Proceeds of the Sale among the Creditors

a. Creditors can file their claims by intervening in the Federal Court action against the vessel (or the proceeds from the sale of the vessel still in Court). They can also institute a separate action against the vessel.
b. Different claims have different priorities in Canada and subject to various exceptions, claims are usually ranked as follows:
First: Maritime liens
Second: Possessory lien

Third: Mortgages
Fourth: Maritime claims entitling a claimant to arrest the vessel but not giving rise to a maritime lien.

c. In the case of foreign vessels all questions of priority of liens or claims are determined by the lex fori.

This can be illustrated by the following case.

In the case of *Todd Shipyards Corporation* v. *Altema Compania Maritima S.A. and the Ship 'IOANNIS DASKALELIS'*, the Supreme Court of Canada in a judgment pronounced December 22, 1972, decided, in establishing priorities with respect to the proceeds from the sale of a Greek vessel sold by Court Order at Vancouver in 1964, that a claim for the cost of shipyard repairs effected in the United States in 1963, which constituted a maritime lien in that country, ranked ahead of a 1961 mortgage registered in Greece.

The Court confirmed that the question as to priority between the claim of the Shipyard and that of the mortgagee must be determined according to the law of Canada, i.e. the lex fori, and that the supplier of such necessaries in Canada is not entitled to a maritime lien under Canadian law. The Court concluded that as a valid maritime lien takes priority over a mortgage, and as the claim for necessary repairs furnished in the United States is recognised as creating that particular kind of lien, the Shipyard's claim should rank ahead of the mortgagee's claim.

It is possible for the creditors by unanimous agreement to decide as to the distribution between themselves of the proceeds of the sale providing such agreement has the approval of the Court.

Appeal Proceedings

There are full rights of appeal with respect to any finding as to priority among creditors, or from any order or judgment of the Court relating to the sale of the vessel.

International Conventions

Canada has not adhered to the 1967 Conventions on Mortgages on Ships and Maritime Liens and Mortgages on Ships under Construction.

Jan Erlund

Denmark

Grounds for an enforced Sale

An enforced sale of a vessel can only be effected by order of the court subsequent to an execution levied on the vessel.

Authority

The bailiff handles the sale.

Care and Maintenance of the Vessel pending Sale

The creditor on whose behalf the sale is made has to arrange for the preservation of the vessel and to advance payment for the expenses incurred in this respect.

Appraisal

In case the creditor and the debtor are unable to agree upon the value of the vessel, an official valuation is made in connection with the enforcement of the judgment.

Notice of Sale

Notice of the sale has to be published in the Danish Gazette six weeks prior to the sale. As regards foreign vessels a further notice has to be published in the state in which the vessel is registered one month prior to the sale. Not later than the day on which the notice of the sale is published in the Danish Gazette the bailiff must notify by registered letter all mortgagees and other holders of registered encumbrances of the sale. In addition the Danish Ships Register must be notified in respect of Danish vessels.

In this connection it must be noted that particulars as to title to the vessel and mortgages on the vessel and other registered encumbrances must be obtained by the bailiff from the Register of the vessel whether Danish or foreign.

Form of actual Sale

An enforced sale can only be effected by public auction.

Minimum Price or any Price

No minimum price is fixed and accordingly the vessel can be sold at any price.

It is possible for the creditors to be present and if necessary protect their interests by buying the vessel themselves.

Provisions regarding credit terms (up to a period of three months) can be included in the written conditions of sale laid down by the bailiff. If such credit terms are not included the purchase price has to be paid in cash and the money must be paid into court.

Distribution of the proceeds

In order to participate in the distribution of the proceeds of the sale the creditors must file their claims in writing.

Danish law recognises

(i) maritime liens
(ii) a right of retention (possessory lien) for claims arising from the building or the repair of the vessel if retained in the possession of the claimants
(iii) mortgages

in the above mentioned priority.

The priority of the maritime liens is established in the Danish Maritime Code (Section 244) in the following order:

1. Wages and other compensation due to the master and the crew members,
2. Harbour dues and costs in connection with pilotage,
3. Claims for compensation due to personal injury arising directly from the operation of the vessel,

4. Claims for damages to property arising directly from the operation of the vessel – provided the claim is not based upon agreement,
5. Salvage remuneration, compensation for removal of wrecks and general average contribution.

The claims listed under 5 rank, however, above the other liens in case the actual claim arises out of an incident of a more recent date than the claims listed under 1 to 4.

The priority of the mortgages is established by the date order of the entries in the ships register of the respective mortgage deeds.

The law of the state of registration of the vessel is applied when determining

- the priority inter se of registered mortgages on a foreign vessel
- the question whether the maritime liens rank above or after the mortgages.

Otherwise lex fori is applied.

The distribution of the proceeds of sale can only be effected by the bailiff. Consequently it is not possible for the creditors by unanimous agreement to decide as to the distribution between themselves of the proceeds of sale.

Appeal Proceedings

An interlocutory appeal can be lodged against the decision (e.g. the distribution of the proceeds) of the bailiff. An application is heard by the Court of Appeal.

International Conventions

Denmark has not adhered to the 1967 Conventions on Mortgages on Ships and Maritime Liens and Mortgages on Ships under Construction.

The provisions of the Conventions are, however, incorporated in the Danish Maritime Code. Denmark is expected to adhere to the Convention in 1976/77.

Other Points of Interest

After an enforced sale of a vessel maritime liens, mortgages and other encumbrances on the vessel are extinguished.

It is a condition for the extinction of the said rights that the buyer has fulfilled the written condition of sale prescribed by the bailiff and that no appeal has been lodged against the bailiff's order of sale within four weeks.

Henrik Langenskiöld

Finland

Grounds for an enforced Sale

Normally an application for the enforced sale of a vessel is based on a final judgment of the Court. In the case of a secured claim based on a mortgage the claimant may invoke the procedure without a judgment. Claims such as those for official harbour dues may be executed without judgment. When the application for an enforced sale is not based on a judgment and a dispute arises the authority concerned must refer such a dispute to the decision of the ordinary Courts.

Authority

An enforced sale of a vessel is handled in the cities by the Magistrate's Court and in the country by the County Court or by the bailiff.

Care and maintenance of the Vessel pending Sale

The party applying for the sale and parties interested in the vessel must take care of the vessel pending the sale. The costs for such a preservation is a first charge on the proceeds of the sale. The authority handling the sale does not have responsibility for the care of the vessel.

Appraisal

The vessel is not appraised by the authority handling the sale prior to the sale of the vessel and the applicant or parties interested in the vessel must therefore handle this matter.

Notice of Sale

Notice of the sale must be published in the official gazette not later than 30 days prior to the sale. In addition notice of the sale must be inserted in a local newspaper on three different occasions, the last one not later than 14 days prior to the sale.

The authority in charge of the sale must obtain from the register of the vessel particulars as to the title to the vessel, particulars of mortgages on the vessel and other registered encumbrances.

The authority must notify the Ships' Register of the pending sale and also send such notices to the mortgagees on the vessel.

Form of actual Sale

The vessel is sold at a public auction.

Minimum Price or any Price

No minimum price is fixed by the authority and accordingly the vessel can be sold at any price obtainable. However, the creditors are free to bid on the vessel and acquire the vessel themselves in order to protect their interests.

Payment of Price

The purchase price must be paid in cash to the authority in charge of the sale within 14 days from the sale. Credit cannot be granted. Mortgages may be taken over with the consent of the other creditors.

Distribution of the Proceeds

The creditors are required to file their claims against the owners of the vessel in writing with the authority in charge of the sale prior to the sale. The claims rank inter se in priority in the following order.

1. Costs for preservation and sale
2. Maritime liens under the 1967 Convention, Article 4 : 1
3. Builders and repairers possessory liens
4. Ships' mortgages

5. General preference for wages of shore personnel in the employment of the shipowner.
6. Other claims.

The validity and priority inter se of registered mortgages is decided by the law of the country where the vessel is registered. All other questions are decided by lex fori.

It is possible for the creditors by unanimous agreement to decide as to the distribution between themselves of the proceeds of sale. It must, however, be noted in this context that the creditors in such a situation are jointly liable to other creditors who have duly filed their claims and who were not present and who did not participate in that decision.

Appeal Proceedings

An appeal can be made to the Courts in respect of the decisions made by the authority in charge of the sale.

International Conventions

Finland has ratified the 1967 Convention.

Jacques Villeneau

France

Grounds for an enforced Sale

A judgment from the Tribunal de Grande Instance is necessary to obtain an enforced sale of a vessel (Article 36 décret of the 27th October 1967).

Authority

According to Article 41 of the décret of the 27th October 1967, the sale should take place at a special hearing of the Tribunal de Grande Instance known as the 'Audience des Criées' (Auction hearing).

According to Article 41, the Court which orders the sale may state that the sale will take place:

(i) Before another Court;
(ii) In the office of and by a 'notaire',
(iii) By a shipbroker; or
(iv) In any part of the port where the ship was arrested.

Care and Maintenance of Vessel pending Sale

According to Article 34 of the décret, at the time of the ship's attachment to the Clerk (huissier) constitutes a custodian. With reference to the law of 19 February 1949, which introduced the rules of the 1926 Convention as to the maritime liens and mortgages, the preservation expenses of the ship, since her last port of call, have a second rank priority among six categories of privileged claims (Art. 31 loi 3–1–1976).

Appraisal

The Court – the Tribunal de Grande Instance – sets out by way of judgment (Article 40) the day and conditions of the sale including the minimum price and also in case there is no bid meeting the minimum price another day for sale on which new bids at a lower minimum price could be accepted.

Notice of Sale

The mortgagees and the other known creditors should be notified prior to the sale (Article 38 décret). The Notice of Attachment must be entered in the Register of Mortgages and on the card kept for each ship by the Customs Authorities if the ship has been registered in France. This must be done within 7 days after attachment. This period can be extended for 20 days if the place of attachment and the Court which is in charge of the sale are not both in Metropolitan France. If the ship is not registered in France, then the Notice is entered in a special Register kept in the Customs' office of the port of arrest (Art. 37 décret).

It should further be noted that Article 38 states that the 'Le Conservateur des Hypotheques Maritimes' (the Officer responsible for the Register of Mortgages) should deliver a record of the known creditors within 7 days of the arrest. This should be announced to the known creditors at their elected domiciles, and should give the day on which they will have to appear before the Court.

Finally it should be noted that Article 41 states that 15 days before the sale a notice must be placed on the mast and advertised in the gazette.

Form of Sale

The vessel must be sold at a public auction. Private sale is not possible.

Minimum Price or any Price

As mentioned above a minimum price is fixed by the judgment which orders the sale and if there is no offer reaching the minimum price, the price is then lowered by the same judgment. A new Public Notice must be made for the second auction.

It is possible for the creditors to be present and if necessary buy the vessel themselves to protect their interests.

Payment of Price

The purchaser must pay the full amount, without any of the expenses which have been incurred, to the 'Caisse de dépots et Consignations' (which is a form of National Trustee bank) within 24 hours of the sale.

Distribution of the Proceeds of Sale

An amicable settlement should try to be achieved. The auctioneer may, within 5 days of the sale, request the President of the Tribunal de Grande Instance to appoint a judge before whom the auctioneer will call the mortgagees to appear within 15 days (Articles 49 and 50 décret).

The creditors with liens and creditors without priority must present their claims to the Tribunal's Record Office within 3 days of the auction (Article 466 décret). If an agreement is reached between all the creditors (known creditors and opposing creditors) the appointed judge will deliver a Notice of Amicable Distribution of the Amount and will order the Record Clerk to issue a 'bordereau de collocation' (Marshalling List).

If there is no agreement, a judicial settlement is necessary. The judge will then issue a Notice of the 'Contredits' (contradictions) of the creditors, each of whom will place, with his title, a request in collocation at the Record Office. At the request of the majority they will be called before the Court which will then deliver the list of collocations. When the judgment is enforced the judge will then give out the list of the collocated credits, with interest. Under his direction the Record Clerk will deliver the individual statements of collocation which are enforceable against the 'Caisse de Dépots et Consignations' (Article 57 décret).

Appeal Proceedings

a. In the case of an amicable settlement the mortgagees may oppose this within 3 days of the sale.
b. In the case of a judicial settlement an appeal may be lodged within 10 days of the notification of the judgment and, this time may be increased, relative to the distance of the place where the sale took place, as in the ordinary rules (Article 53 décret).

International Conventions

France has incorporated the 1926 Convention as to maritime liens and mortgages but not signed the 1967 Conventions in respect of mortgages on ships and maritime liens and mortgages on ships under construction.

Hans-Christian Albrecht

Germany

Grounds for an enforced Sale

As a general rule an enforced sale is ordered by the court on the presentation of an enforceable judgment in favour of the applicant creditor and against the shipowner. There is one exception to this general rule. A notarial deed signed before a German Notary Public, in which the shipowner declares unconditional submission to immediate enforced execution on his property, is also sufficient. Such a deed is often used in connection with mortgages on ships as additional security.

As far as public fees, duties and taxes are concerned and under certain conditions the relevant state authority can issue an order for execution proceedings which then replaces a court judgment.

Authority

The sale is in charge of the lower court (Amtsgericht) at the place where the vessel is berthed. Simultaneously with the order by the court for a forced sale the court also orders the vessel to be seized which order is to be executed by a bailiff.

Care and Maintenance of the Vessel pending Sale

The bailiff who executes the order for seizure is authorised to appoint an official watchman to look after the vessel pending sale. Costs of watchman, harbour dues etc. must be advanced by the applicant creditor but the creditor has a privileged claim for such disbursements on the proceeds of the sale.

Appraisal

No appraisal of the vessel is made prior to the sale.

Notice of Sale

The sale must be published in the German shipping journal *Hansa* and in an official journal at the place of enforced sale and at the port of registry at least six weeks prior to the date of sale.

All creditors known from the ship register (including holders of maritime liens which have been recorded with the ships register during the previous six months) must be – in case of vessels registered in Germany – or shall be – in case of foreign vessels – notified at least 4 weeks prior to sale. Notification by way of official service, which can be effected by special postal delivery and in foreign countries through diplomatic channels.

Notification must mention the place and date of enforced sale and invite creditors with maritime liens to submit substantiation of claim.

A notice of the enforced sale has to be – in case of vessels registered in Germany – or shall be – in case of foreign vessels – sent to the register of the vessel.

The requirements set out above are mandatory.

Form of actual Sale

The sale is handled by a judge or other court official.

In respect of German vessels the ships register sends a complete record to the court handling the sale.

Minimum Price or any Price

In case of vessels registered in Germany bidding must start at a figure which covers all claims preferential to the claim of the creditor who started proceedings and all costs incurred by proceedings (minimum price). Only those claims can be regarded as preferential, which are applied by creditors before time of bidding. No minimum price must be kept where foreign vessels are concerned.

It is possible for the creditors to be present and if necessary protect their interests by buying the vessel themselves.

Payment of Price

The part of the price covering the cost of proceedings and the amount in excess of the minimum bid is due immediately in cash at the auction. For the remainder, arrangements can be made with the other creditors, in particular for renewal of mortgages.

All payment must be made to the court.

Distribution of the Proceeds of Sale

Claims from mortgagees must be substantiated as to the principal amount, interest and costs; other claims, especially those with maritime liens must be authenticated both as to merits and amount (not proof in full, only probability).

Order of preference:

(i) costs of enforced sale proceedings
(ii) maritime liens
(iii) encumbrances according to the ship register, especially mortgages
(iv) non-preferential creditors.

Maritime liens are recognised in the following order of preference:

(i) Claims of the master or any other crew member of a vessel under their articles or contract of employment.
(ii) Public charges to the ship, shipping and port charges, as well as pilotage.
(iii) Claims for compensation as a result of homicide or human injury as well as loss of or damage to things as far as such claims have arisen from the employment of the vessel excluding, however, any such claims for loss or damage to things as are or may be derived from contract, excluding further on any claims resulting from radioactive property or a combination of radioactive property with poisonous, explosive, or other dangerous property of nuclear fuels or radioactive products or waste.
(iv) Costs of salvage and assistance general average contributions by the vessel and the cargo, charges for removing the wreck.
(v) Claims by the different bodies responsible for social security insurance including unemployment insurance.

(This is only a brief summary.)

If all claims filed are subject to the same foreign law or to different foreign laws but with the same priority system, the foreign law will be applied, otherwise German law as lex fori is applied as far as priority is concerned.

It is possible for the creditors by unanimous agreement to decide as to the distribution between themselves of the proceeds of sale.

Appeal Proceedings

It is possible to appeal against the court's order of enforced sale as well as against the manner of distribution of the sale proceeds, in particular when procedural rules have been disregarded.

International Conventions

Germany has not ratified the 1967 Convention in respect of mortgages on ships and maritime liens and mortgages on ships under construction respectively but has already incorporated some parts of the Convention in its national legislation (especially regarding maritime liens).

P. C. Panagopoulos

Greece

Grounds for an unenforced Sale

In principle for an enforced sale a final and conclusive Judgment of a Greek Court is necessary but, also, such sale can take place on the basis of an enforceable title under the relevant provisions of the Greek Code of Civil Procedure, namely:

(i) Final Arbitration Awards

(ii) Court Minutes containing Compromise Settlement or awarding legal costs

(iii) Notarial Deeds

(iv) Orders of Payment issued by Greek Courts

(v) Foreign titles made enforceable in Greece under the relevant provisions of the Greek Code of Civil Procedure. According to Article 6 of the Greek Law referring to Preferred Mortgages, Judgments of foreign Courts regarding liabilities under a preferred mortgage or deed issued by foreign authorities enforceable at their place of issue, may be enforced in Greece even if the Defendant is a Greek subject, without further judicial enquiry by the Greek Court. The order for execution is always issued by the Single Member Court of First Instance.

(vi) Orders and Acts recognised by law as enforceable titles (e.g. the Report in a Public Auction awarding the object of the execution to the higher bidder and the positive declaration of the third person that he is in possession of the object attached).

(vii) *a.* the preferred mortgagee is entitled to sell the vessel without public auction but a clause under which the ownership of the vessel is automatically vested in the preferred mortgagee in case of default is null and void.

b. In case of transfer of the ownership of the vessel in lieu of security the creditor has the right from the moment his secured claim has become due to satisfy himself from the proceeds of the sale of the vessel at a Public Auction.

Authority

The authorities directly involved in the enforced sale are the Court Bailiff and the Notary Public.

The Court participates in the sale if the title should be declared enforceable and in all cases of disputes arising throughout the stage of execution.

In principle the competent Court is the Single Member Court of First Instance.

Care and Maintenance of the Vessel pending Sale

The custodian is appointed at the stage of seizure of the vessel and is usually the person in possession of the vessel at the time of seizure. The competent Magistrate, on the application of any interested party can appoint another custodian or replace same and decide on any dispute regarding these proceedings.

The custodian preserves the vessel seized but has no power to use it. However, following an Order of the Magistrate of the area where the seizure takes place, the custodian can proceed to certain acts of management. He is obligated to account for monies received and must deliver any earnings to the Notary Public appointed for the Public Auction. The Court can appoint as custodian the debtor himself or the creditor. On the other hand the Chief of the Port where the vessel is detained must prevent the vessel from sailing from the moment he is notified of the arrest or seizure of the vessel.

The expenses for the vessel's custody and maintenance for the period from its arrest or seizure until its sale at a Public Auction are considered as legal costs and in view of the fact that they are incurred for the common interest of the creditors are considered as a preferential claim and are included in the first class of the preferential claims giving the right to what may be called a maritime lien under Greek Law.

Appraisal

The attached vessel is valued prior to the enforced sale by the Court Bailiff or by an expert appointed for this purpose at the discretion of the Court Bailiff. The starting price for bids must be not less than half of the valuation price. Against such valuation and fixing of minimum starting price every interested party can file a caveat with the competent Court which has, also, the power to increase the starting price for bids at the Public Auction.

Notice of sale

a. The Court Bailiff instructed to effect the sale must, within fifteen (15) days from the date of the seizure, make out the programme for the Public Auction containing mainly brief description of the vessel seized together with its equipment and appurtenances, a list of the existing mortgages, the name of the creditor and the name of the debtor, the name of the Notary Public who will conduct the Auction, the place, day and time of the auction, the price of the starting bid etc. The said programme is served within twenty (20) days from the date of the seizure on the debtor, on the third party in possession of the vessel (custodian) and on the mortgagees and within the same period a copy is deposited with the Notary Public and a summary thereof is published in a local newspaper of the place of the Auction at least fifteen (15) days prior to the Auction; in case no local daily newspaper is published the programme is posted outside the Port Authority Headquarters at the port of seizure as well as on the vessel in a visible place; within the same period of time a copy of the programme should be served on the Magistrate at the place where the seizure took place. The programme is also served on the Master, on the Chief of the Port where the vessel has been seized and on the Seamen's Pension Fund (N.A.T.).

If the vessel seized in a Greek port is a foreign vessel the Chief of the Port where the seizure took place must send promptly a copy of the Report of Seizure and of the Public Auction programme to the Registrar of the port of registration of the vessel. The same applies in cases of Greek vessels registered in Registries kept by Greek Consular authorities abroad.

b. As explained under *a* above the mortgagees are served with a copy of the programme within twenty (20) days from the date of the seizure and the other unsecured creditors are notified through the publication in the newspaper etc. as outlined under *a* above.

c. No service of the programme is effected on the Registrar of the Port of Registration but only a copy of the Report of the Seizure which must be served within eight (8) days from the date of the seizure.

It follows from the above that particulars as to the title to the vessel and mortgages on the vessel and other registered encumbrances are obtained from the register of the vessel.

Form of actual Sale

The Notary having his seal of office in the area of the Port where the vessel is anchored at the time of the seizure carries out the sale at Public Auction.

Minimum Price or any Price

Further to what is stated above, in principle the sale cannot be concluded below the minimum starting price of the bids. If no bidders turn up at the auction the vessel is awarded to the creditor who has raised execution, upon his request at the starting minimum price. If such request is not submitted, a new public auction will take place within forty (40) days. If during the second public auction no award has been made the Single Member Court of First Instance at the application of an interested party can order a further public auction within thirty (30) days at the same or lower minimum starting price or allow the auction officer (Notary) freely to sell the vessel to the creditor who raised execution or to a third party at a price fixed by the Court, which can also fix the payment of part of the sale price by instalments.

If the third public auction proves fruitless or no free sale of the vessel is effected the Court can lift the seizure or order another public auction at a later time.

It is possible for the creditors to be present and if necessary protect their interest by buying the vessel themselves.

Only the debtor, the Office of the Public Auction (Notary) and his employees are precluded from bidding at the auction. Any creditor can put up a bid unless he is precluded under the provisions of the Greek Civil Code concerning 'conflict of interest' (e.g. the father against the property of his child, the Administrator of an Estate, etc.).

Therefore, a mortgagee can, also, put up bids at the auction.

If the vessel auctioned does not belong to the debtor but to a third party who has mortgaged his vessel in order to provide security for the debtor the third party can put up bids at the auction.

Payment of Price

a. In principle the successful bidder must pay the price in cash as soon as the auction is concluded and the award made. Delivery of the vessel follows the cash payment.

The Notary can allow deferment of payment of part of the price up to fifteen (15) days, but, in this case, he can ask for security (guarantee) from the successful bidder for the fulfilment of his obligations and payment of the balance of the price. In case the successful bidder is a mortgagee the Notary can allow him, up to the time he is definitely classified as a secured creditor, to defer payment of that part of the price corresponding to his claim secured by the mortgage (or a part of it) either with or without the provision of a guarantee.

Moreover it is possible in the auction programme to provide for payment of part of the price and deferment of the balance on credit terms.

It should be noted that the successful bidder, who is also a creditor, has no right to set off the auction price towards his claim against the debtor, because the seizure and the Public Auction are made in favour of the creditor who effected the seizure and pursued the Public Auction. This means that if the vessel is awarded to the pursuer of the seizure and no other creditors have announced themselves the pursuer can set off his claim against the price reached at the auction.

From the moment the successful bidder has been awarded the vessel he is liable for its loss or damage even before he has taken delivery of the vessel.

b. The price is paid as specified above to the Notary who is obligated to deposit the money after the conclusion of the auction with the Deposits and Loans Fund, a Government Institution. The cashier will pay the money to the persons indicated by the Notary. It should be noted that the cashier of the Fund is not considered a third party and therefore no attachment of the auction price can be effected in his hands.

Distribution of the Proceeds of the Sale

The distribution is initiated:

a. by an 'announcement' which takes the form of a legal document containing amongst others the names of the creditor and debtor, description of the claim the precise facts and legal basis of the claim the appointment of an agent to receive substituted service of process residing in the area of the Magistrates Court where execution takes place and the demand for payment; it must be signed by an Advocate; it is not necessary for it to be addressed to the debtor, but, it must be served on him, as well as on the Notary and on the person who has instituted the seizure and the Public Auction.

The 'announcement' must be served within five (5) days from the auction and service of the same can take place even on a Sunday; within the same time (5 days) the creditor must deposit with the Notary all the documents evidencing his claim. The expenses are borne by the person who announces himself as a creditor. Omission to effect all the above services may invalidate the announcement but only in case of detriment caused to the person who raises the objection.

The debtor has the right to file a 'caveat' against the 'announcement' up to the day of the distribution of the auction price; copy of the caveat is served promptly on the Notary, who cannot proceed to the payment of the claims, to those creditors whose 'announcement' has been attacked by the caveat. The Court which deals with the said caveat may, at the request of the Defendant-Creditor order the Notary to pay the claim against adequate security (guarantee) provided by the Defendant-Creditor.

Within three (3) days from the date when the list of classification of the creditors is prepared, the Notary invites in writing the creditor who effected the seizure and Public Auction, the debtor and the announced creditors to inspect the list. Within eight (8) days from the service of the above invitation every interested party can file a caveat against the list of classification copy of which is served within the same time on the Notary and is directed against the creditors whose classification is disputed, as to the class, amount and validity of claim etc.

b. Doctrine of priorities

All claims have not the same rank. The types of claim may be distinguished according to their ranking.

I. *Maritime privileges or Liens*

According to the Greek Code of Private Maritime Law certain claims are privileged or give a right to what we can call a 'statutory maritime lien' attaching to the ship and the freight and rank as follows irrespective of the time they were created:

(i) Legal costs incurred in the common interest of the creditors, dues and charges to which the ship is subject, the taxes relevant to the navigation as well as the expenses for the custody and maintenance of the ship from her arrival at the last port.

(ii) Claims arising from the contracts of employment of Master and crew as well as the contributions due to the Seamen's Pension Fund accruing from the employment of the crew.

(iii) Expenses and awards arising from assistance at sea and salvage.

(iv) Indemnities due to ships, passengers or cargo by reason of collision of ships.

Privileged claims of the same rank are distributed rateably. In case of several claims arising from assistance at sea and salvage, latter claims have precedence over prior claims.

In the case of contractual sale of the ship, the privilege (lien) continues to attach, provided the same is admitted by a Court Judgment against the transferee of the ship, through a lawsuit which must be brought within three (3) months from the date of registration of the contract of sale in the Register Book of Ships. The above privileges (liens) are extinguished by the enforced sale of the ship and cannot be enforced against the insurance indemnity.

The person claiming a privilege (lien) can also apply for the arrest (or preventive seizure) of the ship in the hands of the transferee. On the other hand, if the privileged creditor has an enforceable title against the original debtor he can proceed within the same three-month period against the transferee without filing a lawsuit for Judgment recognising and admitting his claim.

II. *Maritime Mortgages*

Next rank the maritime mortgages provided they have been registered prior to the registration of a seizure, and in accordance with their priority depending on the date of their registration. It is immaterial whether the mortgage is a preferred one or not.

III. Next rank claims which are secured by the transfer of the ownership in the ship in lieu of security. The creditor in question is entitled to be paid off from the proceeds of the enforced sale of the ship at Public Auction and ranks after the mortgagees.

IV. Finally all the other announced creditors are satisfied pro rata in case the auction price is not sufficient to satisfy all claims in full.

c. In principle the law of the flag is applied provided it is not contrary to Greek Public Policy. A mortgage (whether ordinary or preferred) attaching to a ship at the time when the ship acquired the Greek flag, remains in full force, provided under the law of the preceding flag it was recorded by its entry in a public registry and was subsequently entered in the Greek Register of Mortgages within sixty (60) days after the registration of the ship in the Greek Registry.

According to express provision in the Greek Code of Maritime Law (article 9) all rights attaching to a ship are governed by the law of its flag. The matter of priorities in the classification of creditors is a matter of substantive and not procedural law, according to Greek Law, and therefore the lex fori is not applied.

In principle, it is possible for the creditors by unanimous agreement to decide as to the distribution between themselves of the proceeds of sale provided that such agreement is not contrary to Greek Public Policy as would be the case if such agreement violates for instance the provisions relating to privileged creditors.

Appeal Proceedings

The various lawsuits relating to execution in general may refer *a* to the validity of the title, *b* to the validity of the procedure followed and *c* to the validity and substance of the claim.

The lawsuits are conducted in the form of 'caveats' before the Single Member Court of the place where execution is raised.

The caveat under *a* above should be filed with fifteen (15) days from the date of the Report of the Seizure; in the cases under *b* and *c* above it should be filed up to the commencement of making the report on the Public Auction and the award to the successful bidder. Finally if the caveat refers to the validity of the award it should be filed within ninety (90) days from the date of registration of the award of the auction in the Register of Vessels.

A third party claiming a right attaching to the vessel can, also, file a caveat against both creditor and debtor and record it in the Register Book of Vessels.

In the above law suits regarding execution any creditor of the debtor can intervene.

In principle the time limits set for the lawsuits regarding execution as well as the filing of such caveats do not suspend the execution of the Court Judgment. However, at the request of the person who files the caveat, the Court, considering that the execution might cause to the applicant irreparable damage, may suspend execution without any condition or against proper security or allow the execution to proceed against proper security given by the creditor who has raised the execution.

Although strictly not an Appeal, mention should be made here of the right of the debtor to apply to the competent Court for suspension of the Public Auction. The suspension may be granted with or without condition (such as payment of part of the debt) and cannot be granted for a period of more than three (3) months.

International Conventions

Greece has not adhered to the Brussels Convention of 1926 regarding Mortgages on Ships and Maritime Liens but certain provisions of this Convention have been adopted by the new Code of Private Maritime Law (Law No. 3816/1958) under the sections Mortgages on Ships and Privileged Claims (Maritime Lien). Article 195 of the said Code makes it possible to register a maritime mortgage on a ship under construction, provided she is registered.

Otherwise no other Convention on the subjects in question has been ratified or adopted by Greece.

Greece will certainly adhere to and ratify the 1967 Convention in respect of mortgages and maritime items and mortgage on ships under construction in the not too distant future.

Other points of Interest

(i) It should be noted that an enforced sale at Public Auction is always preceded by the 'seizure' of the vessel on the basis of an enforceable title which must be final and conclusive.

The seizure cannot be effected before the lapse of twenty-four hours from the service of the writ calling upon the debtor to effect immediate payment of the claim.

Where the vessel is in the possession of a third person, the execution is brought against the debtor but the writ for payment is served, also, under penalty of nullity of the proceedings, upon the third party and in his absence, upon the Master.

The writ for payment can be served upon the Master if the claim is connected with the operation of the vessel or is preferred (lien) or is secured by mortgage.

The report of the seizure mentions the name, profession and home address of the creditor, the enforceable title, the writ for payment served upon the debtor or upon the third party or the Master, the demand for seizure, the amount of the claim, the appointment by the creditor of an agent to receive substituted service of process at the place where seizure takes place, the name of the shipowner and the Master, description of the vessel and other data of the same and the appointment of a watchman.

This report is served *a* on the debtor, at the end of the seizure if he was present, but, if he refuses to accept it then the Court Bailiff makes a report about this refusal; if the debtor was not present or it is not possible to prepare the copy of the report or a summary thereof forthwith, service is effected at the latest within the following day from the date of seizure, if he resides in the area where the seizure took place, otherwise within eight (8) days from the date of the seizure; *b* on the third party owning or in possession of the vessel within the said eight (8) days; *c* on the Registrar of the Port where the vessel is registered (in the case of foreign vessels see under (*a*) above) within the same eight (8) days; *d* on the Chief of the Port Authority where the seizure took place within two (2) days from the date of the seizure and *e* on the Notary appointed as the Officer to carry out the Public Auction within fifteen (15) days from the date of the seizure.

(ii) The expenses connected with the enforced sale are eventually borne by the debtor but are prepaid by the creditor who started the execution.

(iii) By payment of the auction price all mortgages and other burdens and charges are extinguished.

(iv) The mortgagee may agree that the successful bidder takes the ship subject to the continuation of the mortgage on the ship; this arrangement is recorded in the Report of the Award of the Public Auction; in that case the successful bidder does not pay the part of the auction price corresponding to the claim of the mortgagee.

(v) Claims to ownership of the ship sold at the public auction must be exercised through a lawsuit to be filed within five (5) years from the date of the registration of the Auction Award to the successful bidder; otherwise the said claims become statute-barred.

Gerald J. Moloney

Ireland

Grounds for an enforced Sale

In general it is necessary to have a judgment from a Court as a basis for an enforced sale but such a sale can also be effected on the basis of an application to the Court by a private individual.

Authority

An enforced sale is handled by the Court.

Care and Maintenance of the Vessel pending Sale

After arrest of the vessel by the Admiralty Marshal he arranges for its preservation pending the order of the Court for the sale and this order provides for preservation of the vessel pending sale. The expenses of preservation (together with the expenses of arrest) become a claim on the proceeds of sale in priority to everything other than the expenses of sale.

Appraisal

It is the practice of the Court to have a valuation made.

Notice of Sale

Publication of Notice is a matter for the Court ordering the sale.

Notice is normally ordered by the Court to be given to Mortgagees and such Creditors as notify their claims to the Court. In addition it is most probable that the Court will also order notification to be given to known Creditors who have not claimed. It is a matter for the Court to decide the means and time of notification.

Normally the Court obtains from the Register of the vessel such information which is available as to title to the vessel and other registered encumbrances.

Form of actual Sale

The sale is handled by an Auctioneer appointed by the Court.

Minimum Price or any Price

It is a matter for the Court to decide the price at which the vessel is to be sold. It would normally have regard to any valuation which had been obtained, any representations which might be made by any person having an interest in the vessel and is made privately by the Court.

It is possible for the Creditors to be present and if necessary protect their interest by buying the vessel themselves.

Payment of Price

While the terms of the sale are primarily a matter for the Court it is thought very unlikely that the Court would allow payment to be made otherwise than in cash except with the express consent of the Creditors or of a majority of them.

All payments are made to the Court.

Distribution of the Proceeds

Distribution of the proceeds is made in the order of priorities referred to hereunder to such Creditors as have pursued their claim to judgment in separate actions.

The Irish Courts have taken the same system of priorities as England with one difference and that is the question of foreign mortgages on foreign ships arrested and sold in Ireland. In 1972 the Irish High Court decided to give priority according to the Register to a German mortgage on a German ship (which mortgage was registered in the German Register). On appeal the Supreme Court, by a majority, upheld the decision. In this regard it should be noted that once the mortgage is 'registered' it takes priority. Under the Irish Shipping Act 1955 only a mortgage on an Irish ship can be 'registered'.

It is believed that no objection would be raised by the Court to all Creditors who were parties to proceedings regarding the sale of a ship and the distribution of the proceeds, or notice parties to such proceedings, compromising the proceedings on any *agreed* basis of distribution.

Appeal Proceedings

There is only one Local Admiralty Court – in Cork – and an appeal would lie from this Court to the High Court. Such an appeal is a rehearing. If the Court of original jurisdiction is the High Court an appeal would lie to the Supreme Court on a point of law only.

International Conventions

Ireland has not signed or otherwise into Irish law incorporated international Conventions affecting enforced sales of vessels.

Other Points of Interest

The Irish Admiralty Law is very much out of date and the attitude of the Courts seems to be to follow the English practice in so far as it is possible to do so under the slightly different laws operating in this country.

The Judge of the Cork Local Admiralty Court has for the past two years or so declined to exercise his Admiralty Jurisdiction on the grounds that such jurisdiction is possibly unconstitutional. An appeal to the Supreme Court was made about two years ago and dismissed on a technical point without the constitutional issue having been decided.

Attilio Costabel

Italy

Grounds for an enforced Sale

The Code of Navigation (Royal Decree 30th March, 1942, n. 327) provides for a special procedure for enforcement in respect of ships. Such procedure differs in some ways from the normal one following the Code of Civil Procedure.

The enforced sale of a ship is a stage of that procedure, and must be preceded by many formalities, which are a condition precedent.

A so called 'enforceable title' (like a final judgment, or a protested cheque or bill of exchange, etc.) is necessary for proceeding to the enforcement, contrary to the 'arrest' of the ship, which can be, and is normally given before such an enforceable title is in existence.

When a ship is under arrest, the Creditor can ask for her sale after obtaining an enforceable title.

The first act of the enforcement procedure is the service made by the creditor to the debtor, through the Court Bailiff, of the enforceable title, accompanied by an intimation to pay within 24 hours ('precetto').

If the debtor does not do so, the creditor can proceed to the next step, the seizure of the ship. This must be done not later than 30 days from the service of the 'precetto', failing which a new 'precetto' must be served.

The seizure is effected by serving on the Shipowner and on the Master through the Bailiff an act containing the description of the enforceable title, the date of the service of the 'precetto', an intimation to the debtor not to sell the ship or anyway dispose of it, and to the Master not to let the ship sail, and finally the ship's description (name, registration number, tonnage, etc.). A copy of the service, when completed, is sent, by the creditor, to the Port Authority where the ship is registered, and the seizure is recorded in the Registry and in the ship's books. A certificate of such record is given by the Port Authority to the creditor.

Authority

The enforcement is directed by a judge of the 'Tribunale' (Court of first instance) if the ship is one licensed for high seas trade, or by a judge of the 'Pretura' (Lower Court of first instance) if the ship is licensed for coastal navigation only.

The judge territorially competent is the one of the port where the ship lies, at the time of the enforcement.

An order of the judge is necessary for proceeding to the sale. Such order (as in detail described below) is obtained upon request of the creditor, in the form of a request addressed to the competent judge.

The request cannot be filed until 30 days have elapsed from the date of the seizure, but not after 90 days from such date.

The request must be served, through the Bailiff, on the Shipowner, on the Mortgagees and on other creditors who may have intervened in the enforcement procedure, inviting them to submit their comments upon the conditions of the sale.

After the service, the request, together with an abstract of the ship's registration, showing the mortgages entered, must be deposited with the clerk of the competent judge.

Such deposit must be made within 30 days from the service of the request of sale, but always within 90 days from the date of the seizure of the ship.

The clerk opens an official file, in which are inserted also a copy of the seizure act, the Port Authority document certifying the record of the seizure in the registry, and the comments if any on the conditions of the sale by the interested parties. The President of the Tribunal (or of the Lower Court) then appoints one specific judge to follow and direct the sale, and at the same time appoints an expert to estimate the value of the vessel.

Care and Maintenance of the Vessel pending Sale

The Authorities in charge of the sale are not supposed to, and do not, take care of the vessel pending sale.

The creditor himself must take action in his own interests or, if several creditors are proceeding to enforcement, action can be taken by one or several or all of them in the common interest.

However, any costs or expenditure incurred for such actions rank in priority before any lien or mortgage (such priority is given to any costs incurred for the care and the maintenance of the ship pending enforced sale, irrespective of who incurred such costs). The Code of

Navigation provides for a special procedure of ship's management judicially controlled pending sale, which, however, should not be confused with ordinary care and maintenance pending sale.

Such procedure can be allowed by the judge at the request of one or several creditors, in particular circumstances, and consists in letting the ship perform one or several voyages, under strict control of the Court, and not without suitable insurance of the ship having been arranged.

The costs for insurance and all other costs must be advanced by the creditors who requested this procedure and rank in priority as a first charge on the proceeds of the sale. The net freights earned are distributed to the creditors.

During such procedure, a caretaker can be appointed to look after the ship and to receive requests and complaints. He is, nevertheless, not bound to nor supposed to advance any funds out of his own pocket (though if he does, of his own volition, his credit will rank in first priority, together with any other costs for similar actions taken by creditors or any other party concerned). It is debated whether a caretaker can be appointed also when that special procedure of 'controlled management' of the ship is not carried out.

The Code is silent on the point, but nothing prevents the creditors from applying to the judge, who may decide to the circumstances.

Appraisal

The appraisal of value of the vessel is done by an expert appointed by the Court, and is taken as the basic offer for the bids.

The estimate must be deposited by the expert within a period of time stated by the judge, which cannot exceed 30 days.

The deposit of the estimate by the expert is the last preliminary act before the enforced sale, which takes place as follows.

Notice of Sale

The enforced sale cannot be done without the Court order having been properly notified and publicised. The order is issued by the judge appointed to direct the sale, not before five days from the deposit of the expert's estimate.

The judge must also hear the Shipowner, the creditor who is proceeding, the mortgagees and the other creditors who may have intervened before the order was issued.

The order describes the ship in all details, and contains the following indications:

- the basic offer (which is the expert's estimate);
- the date and hour of the auction;
- the amount of the deposit that must be advanced by the bidders (10% of the basic price, plus estimated cost of the auction and of the fiscal registration of ship's property's transfer, etc.);
- the minimum increase of the bids;
- the terms and modes of payment of the price (payment that, in any case, cannot be done later than 60 days from the sale).

The order is notified by the clerk to the Shipowner, the proceeding creditor, the mortgagees and the creditors who may have intervened. Such notice is not necessary, however, for those parties who were heard by the judge before issuing the order.

The order is also recorded in the seizure act, in the Tribunal's file; is published in the legal bans and is exposed to the public in a special place of the Court.

The judge may also order other forms of notice, like publication in newspapers.

Form of actual Sale

It is expressly stated by the Code of Navigation that the enforced sale must be done, in a first instance, in the form of the public auction, with the 'candle' system (a certain number of candles are lit, in progression, while bids are made, and the winning bid is the highest at the moment of the extinguishing of the last candle).

Minimum Price or any Price

If no offers are made, even at the minimum price, the judge orders new auctions, reducing, from time to time, the basic offer by 20%. When the basic offer goes down to 40% of the original one as per the expert's estimate, without still any offer, the judge, after hearing the interested parties, orders a sale by private treaty, laying down the terms and conditions.

Both at the auction and at the private treaty, offers can be made by any interested party, creditors included, either directly or through special power of attorney.

Only the Shipowner debtor is not admitted to bid.

Payment of Price

The person whose bid has been accepted must pay the amount of his bid, less the deposit made, in the form and in the time stated by the judge in the order of sale.

Distribution of the Proceeds of Sale

This aspect of the enforced sale of the ship is governed by the normal rules of civil procedure.

If there is only one creditor in the procedure, the judge, after hearing the debtor, orders payment to the creditor of all moneys due to him for capital, interest and costs.

If more than one creditor are proceeding or have filed intervention, the judge, not later than 30 days from the payment of price, delivers a project of distribution, listing the creditors in their rank of priorities.

Such project is deposited with the judge's clerk where it can be perused by the creditors and the debtor.

The judge also arranges for a hearing in respect of the project, giving all parties a notice of at least 10 days.

The party not appearing at the hearing is considered as having approved the project.

If the project is approved, the judge orders payment of the shares. If instead any dispute arises about the existence or the amount of one or more claims, or about preferential claims, the judge proceeds to collect evidence and to decide, along the normal procedure rules (if he is competent, otherwise he orders the parties to resume their case before the competent judge, within a specific term). The judge, as he thinks advisable, may suspend the distribution of the moneys collected, or may order distribution of the undisputed amounts.

The distribution is made following the rank of priorities, as determined by the 1926 Convention on Liens and Mortgages on Ships (ratified by Italy) whenever applicable, or by the Code of Navigation Rules, which basically follow the Convention.

The list of the priorities stated by the Code of Navigation is the following:

Maritime liens rank before mortgages, and mortgages rank before civil law liens.

Maritime liens, in their turn, rank in the following order:

(1) Law costs due to the State and expenses incurred in the common interest of the creditors for the enforcement procedure or for obtaining security, port, harbour and anchorage dues and other

similar charges, pilotage dues, costs for care and maintenance of the ship in the last port.

(2) Claims arising out of contracts of engagement of the master and crew.

(3) Crew repatriation and maintenance expenses incurred or estimated to be incurred by the Merchant Marine or Consular Authorities; social contributions for the seamen.

(4) Remuneration and costs for salvage; general average contributions.

(5) Indemnities for collision or other accidents of navigation, indemnities for damage to port structures and docks; indemnities for death and personal injury of passengers or crew; indemnities for loss of or damage to cargo or baggage.

(6) Claims arising from contracts entered into by the Master for the care of the ship or prosecution of the voyage (this subsection refers to a very particular procedure foreseen by the Code of Navigation, concerning the case the Master is in need of financing for the above purposes, at a port where the Shipowner is not physically present or represented. In practice such a situation does not occur any more).

The liens arising out of the last voyage rank prior to the ones of the preceding voyage, except claims arising out of a contract of engagement extending for more than one voyage, all rank within claims attaching to the last voyage. The claims mentioned in each of the above numbers compete in proportion of their amounts, if the proceeds of the sale are not enough to satisfy them in full.

In such a case, however, there are a few exceptions. Out of the claims under No. (5) the indemnities for death or personal injury rank before the ones for loss of or damage to goods. The claims listed in Nos. (4) and (6) rank in inverse priority in respect of the date when each of them came into existence. The claims arising from the same cause or event are considered as arisen contemporaneously.

The Code of Navigation explicitly foresees that liens and mortgages and any other similar rights 'in rem' (as well as, of course, the rights of property, and the relevant formalities and publicity) are governed by the law of the ship's flag.

This provision does not give liberty to the parties to dispose otherwise, for no choice is available for other laws like the one of the country where the specific lien arose, or the lex fori etc.

Foreign vessels can be subject to enforced sale in Italy, and the above rules will apply, for the basic principle that procedure matters are governed by the lex fori.

Of course any question concerning the merits will be governed by the law applicable, along the normal conflict of law rules with the exception mentioned above.

Appeal Proceedings

Oppositions can be filed against the enforced sale, based upon various grounds.

The opposition can be against the alleged right of the creditor to proceed to enforcement, or against a formal irregularity of the title or of the single acts of enforcement. The latter kind of opposition must be filed in a short term of five days.

Third parties claiming ownership over the vessel can also file opposition at any time, but not after the sale is ordered by the judge.

International Conventions

The Conventions ratified by Italy are: The Brussels Convention of 10/4/1926 on liens and mortgages on ships, and the Brussels Convention of 10/4/1926 on the immunities of State-owned Ships. The 1967 Conventions on liens and mortgages on ships under construction have not yet been ratified.

Other Points of Interest

It may be interesting to mention that certain immunities are stated by the Code of Navigation.

Ships of war cannot be seized.

The ships employed in lines declared by Merchant Marine Ministry to be of public interest, or employed in public service on inland waterways, cannot be seized without previous authority of the Ministry of Merchant Marine.

Ships which have obtained from the Port Authority the sailing clearance (so called 'ready to sail') cannot be seized, unless for credits concerning the particular voyage to be commenced.

Yoichi Ogawa

Japan

Grounds for an enforced Sale

There are two categories of enforced sales. The one is made pursuant to such 'title of obligation' as a judgment of the court against the Owners of the vessel, a compromise and an admission of the claim entered in the court record and a deed drawn by a notary public stating therein that the Owner of the vessel has no objection to the immediate execution.

The other is made by an application by mortgagees or those who have a maritime lien or possessory lien on the vessel for an order for sale without obtaining a judgment.

Note: Execution on a *foreign judgment* may be effected only when its lawfulness is admitted by a 'judgment for execution' by a Japanese Court. A judgment for execution is to be given without looking into the merits of the case but on condition that the jurisdiction of the foreign court is not denied under the Japanese laws or treaties, the defendant, being a Japanese citizen, has been properly summoned or appeared before the court, the judgment is not contrary to Japanese public policy and there is a mutual assistance on a reciprocal basis in the execution of the judgment.

Note: Execution on *Arbitration award* may be effected only when the execution is allowed by a 'judgment for execution' by the court. A 'judgment for execution' is to be given without looking into the merits of the case but on condition that arbitration procedure is not prohibited in the particular case, the performance awarded is not illegal and the parties have been properly represented in the procedure and properly heard.

Authority

The sale is handled by the district court that has jurisdiction over the port of registry or the court within the jurisdiction of which the vessel is lying.

Care and Maintenance of the Vessel pending Sale

Upon commencement of the auction proceedings, entry of the application for the enforced sale is made in the register by which the arrest of the vessel comes into effect. After such registration is made third parties are not able to effectively obtain any right on the vessel which may prejudice the creditors.

Upon commencement of the enforced sale proceeding, the vessel is ordered to stay by the court and the court shall, upon motion of the creditor, issue an order to the court marshal to watch and preserve the vessel. The court marshal ordinarily requests assistance for preservation which the applicant has practically to arrange. The expenses necessary for the preservation shall be advanced by the applicant to the court.

Appraisal

The court shall appoint a proper expert to appraise the vessel after receiving notice from the register officer that an application for enforced sale has been made. If the court considers the valuation improper, the court may order further appraisal.

Notice of Sale

a. Service of the decision of the commencement of the enforced sale proceedings shall be given to the debtor (Shipowner), if the debtor (Shipowner) is a foreign citizen, such service is made through diplomatic channels, but the court, upon motion of the applicant or at its discretion may serve by way of service by publication which comes into effect upon elapse of a period of 6 weeks. The service by publication is made by similar procedure as the public notice described in 3.

b. Notice of the commencement of the enforced sale proceedings is given by the court to the applicant, registered mortgagees, registered demise charterers and tax authorities. If the person to receive notice is in a foreign country, the notice is not necessarily given.

c. The notice of the date of auction and the date of the determination of the successful bidder is given by way of a public notice on the notice board of the court and the local administrative authority. The notice may also be given in one or more newspapers by discretion of the court. If the vessel to be auctioned is in a place other than the port of registry, the notice is given by the court that has jurisdiction over the port of registry.

The notice shall be given at least 14 days prior to the date of auction and the date of the determination of the successful bidder shall be fixed within 7 days after the date of auction.

The following items shall be included in the above notice.

1. Principal particulars of the vessel.
2. Taxes incurred.
3. Registered demise charter.
4. The statement that the auction is to be carried out by virtue of the execution.
5. Time, date and place of the auction.
6. The minimum price.
7. Time, date and place of the determination of the successful bidder.
8. The place where execution record may be perused.
9. The statement that the persons holding maritime lien shall notify the claim to the court.
10. The statement that any interested parties shall appear on the date of auction.

Form of actual Sale

The sale will be conducted by the court marshal at a public auction where anybody is entitled to participate and bid for the vessel. In the case of a sale of a Japanese registered ship, no foreigner can participate.

The court may, upon motion of the interested parties or on its own authority, order sale by tender instead of public auction. Such order shall be given prior to the public notice of the date of auction. In such a case the tendered prices are not known to the other participants until the court marshal has opened the sealed tenders and accordingly it is possible to say that a relatively high price would be expected.

Extract of the register of the vessel or other records showing title, encumbrances, mortgage holders etc. will be available at the court.

Minimum Price or any Price

The minimum price is fixed by the court based on the expert's appraisal. The minimum price cannot be changed even by the agreement of all parties concerned.

In case no bid is given on better terms than the minimum price so fixed, the court may reconsider the minimum price subject to such new price being able to cover the costs of the proceedings including the maintenance and preservation expenses plus all claims with higher preference than the claim of the applicant.

In case the court deems that the minimum price would not cover the costs of the proceedings including the maintenance and preservation expenses plus all claims with higher preference than the claim of the applicant, the court shall notify it to the applicant. Unless the applicant himself within 7 days offers to buy at a fixed price not less than the amount to cover the above and furnishes the court with sufficient security, the enforced sale is cancelled by the court.

Payment of Price

a. One tenth (1/10) of the offered price shall be deposited in cash or negotiable instrument (valuation of which will be subject to the court marshal and much lower than the market price) by all bidders. The deposit is not returned until after the successful bidder has been determined or the enforced sale proceedings have been cancelled.

The remaining 9/10 of the price shall be paid in principle in cash to the court on the date determined by the court. Negotiable instruments deposited are encashed at the market price.

b. Instead of a cash payment, the successful bidder may assume encumbrances on the vessel and debt and obligation owned by the debtor with consents of other creditors.

c. By the payment of the price, the successful bidder will obtain the ownership of the vessel free from all and any encumbrances except the possessory lien of builders or repairers and the registered demise charter for a period of not more than 6 months.

Distribution of the Proceeds of Sale

The proceeds are distributed by the court at the date fixed by the court at which time all creditors are heard.

Demands for distribution are to be made to the court until the close of the date of auction and the court notifies such demands to the parties concerned.

If a demand is made by a creditor without having a title of obligation, the debtor (Shipowner) has to answer whether he admits such claim or not within 3 days after his receiving notice for such demand; failing to do so, such claim is deemed to be admitted by the debtor.

If such claim is denied, the creditor shall commence a suit for establishing the claim within 3 days after the denial.

The priorities between claims are shortly as follows:

1. Costs for the sale including costs for preservation and maintenance of the vessel.
2. Maritime lien under the law of the flag.
3. Ship's mortgage.
4. National and local taxes and dues.

   (*Note*) In case the registration of a mortgage was entered after the due date of taxes and dues, such taxes and dues have priority over such mortgage.
5. Other claims.

As to the maritime lien, although there is no well established precedent authority, the law of the flag would usually be applied but there is a possibility of application of Japanese law in case that the act out of which the claim arises was done in Japan.

Maritime liens under Japanese law are as follows:

1. Costs for the enforced sale including expenses for preservation of the vessel and its equipment after commencing the sale proceedings.
2. Expenses for preservation of the vessel and its equipment at the last port.
3. All public dues in respect of the voyage.
4. Pilotage and tug boat charge.
5. Salvage charge and vessel's general average contribution.
6. Expenses necessary to continue the voyage.
7. Crew wages.
8. Claims arising out of sale, construction and rigging of the vessel in case the vessel has not yet sailed on any voyage after the sale or construction. Claims in respect of supplying food and fuel and rigging for the last voyage.
9. Claims, against which the shipowner is able to limit liability.

Dispute between creditors regarding the distributors of proceeds is adjudged by the court. Such portion of distribution that is not in dispute is paid regardless of the dispute.

Appeal Proceedings

Objections can be made against the enforced sale at any stage from the decision of the commencement of the enforced sale until the payment of purchase money by the successful bidder on the ground of either the procedure being improper, non-existence of right of execution expressed in the title of obligation or the vessel being owned by a third party. Even if such objection is made, the sale proceedings continue unless the court orders a stay of proceedings. An objection can also be made against the court's permission of sale within 7 days from the date of such permission and the procedure is suspended. An objection can also be made against distribution of the proceeds but the distribution is not suspended unless the court orders a stay upon motion.

International Conventions

Japan has not ratified the 1926 and the 1967 Convention on maritime liens and mortgages.

Other Points of Interest

1. A vessel ready to sail cannot be arrested unless the claimants' claim is arising out of the preparation of the commencement of the voyage.
2. The voyage stopped by arrest can be permitted by the court upon motion of the debtor with the agreement of all the interested parties in the case that it deemed appropriate for commercial interests.
3. The enforced sale of a share of a vessel may be done by the court that has a jurisdiction over the port of registry without arresting the vessel.
4. There is no provision of a period within which the enforced sale shall be concluded and very approximately it takes about 3–4 months from the time of the application of the enforced sale until the time of the auction subject to the court congestion and numbers of objections made.
5. Amendment of the law of the enforced sale of vessel is now under consideration.

R. Farrugia

Malta

Grounds for an enforced Sale

A creditor can effect an enforced sale of a vessel if –

a. he has in his favour a registered mortgage – for such a sale there are no rules as the Merchant Shipping Act gives to the creditor 'power absolutely to sell the ship', though normally it is advisable that the procedure of judicial sales by auction be adopted; or

b. he has an 'executive title' in which case a judicial sale by auction can be made under the provisions of the Code of Organisation of Civil Procedure.

'Executive titles' are Court judgments, notarial deed for a debt certain liquidated and due, taxed bills of costs and arbitration awards.

Authority

The judicial sale is ordered by a decree of the Court (normally the Commercial Court), which decree is to be served on the debtor. A second decree will then appoint the place and date for the effective sale and a licensed auctioneer to hold the auction sale. Such decree will also be served on the debtor and on the consignatory if any.

Care and Maintenance of the Vessel pending Sale

Unless there is agreement between the parties, the Court will give all the necessary orders for the preservation of the vessel in the interests of all concerned. The relative expenses shall be a first charge on the proceeds of the sale, but initially and provisionally they are to be met by the party demanding the sale.

Valuation

A valuation is not necessary, but the Court will order a valuation 'if required by the creditor or by the debtor'.

Notice of Sale

The advertisement of the sale shall be posted at the Court buildings and published in the Government Gazette. The Court can 'order such advertisement to be published in one or more periodical newspapers'.

There is no statutory requirements about particulars as to title to the vessel and mortgages. Such data usually would result during the proceedings and normally the creditor and the persons charged with the sale tend to check such information. When there are competing claims such particulars necessarily emerge.

Form of actual Sale

Normal auction proceedings. Bids are to be made orally. Each bid is to be announced at least three times unless a higher bid is previously made. The highest bidder, with the time stated in the advertisement, shall be the purchaser. The creditor can bid.

Minimum Price or any Price

No minimum price is fixed, but the sale is not effected if there be less than three bidders.

Payment of Price

The price is to be paid in cash under the authority of the Court.

The Court may authorise a creditor to bid 'animo compensandi'. In such a case the purchaser is to demand the approval of the set-off and pay only the surplus, if any.

Distribution of the Proceeds

Claims on the proceeds are to be made by an application (which in itself has the effect of a garnishee order). If there is no agreement between the various claimants in respect of eventual priorities (arising out of hypothecs, heirs, privileges, mortgages etc.) the matter will be decided by the competent Court.

Appeal Proceedings

Any judgment of the Court of first instance (and in maritime matters such court is the Commercial Court) are subject to appeal before the Court of Appeal. Some orders (decrees not being decrees during a suit) can be only contested by a Writ of Summons before the Court of first instance, but the judgment on such contestation is subject to the normal appeal proceedings.

International Conventions

Malta has not adhered to any international Convention in respect of the enforced sales of ships.

F. Baron van der Feltz

The Netherlands

Grounds for an enforced Sale

Judgments or orders from the Courts are necessary for an enforced sale of vessels. There is one exception. An enforced sale can be made on the basis of a mortgage deed executed before a Netherlands Notary Public.

Authority

The Court of first instance or a Notary Public handles the sale.

Care and Maintenance of the Vessel pending Sale

The person who has arrested the vessel has to take care of the vessel and also pay the expenses for the preservation of the vessel.

Appraisal

No appraisal is made.

Notice of Sale

A 20 days' notice is required prior to the sale. The mortgagees and other known creditors must be given 20 days' notice prior to the sale by a warrant of execution.

No notice of the enforced sale is sent to the register of the vessel.

It is required that particulars as to title to the vessel and mortgages on the vessel and other registered encumbrances are obtained from the register of the vessel.

Form of actual Sale

The sale is handled by the Court in the form of a public auction.

Minimum Price or any Price

No minimum price is fixed and accordingly the vessel can be sold at any price.

It is possible for the creditors to be present and if necessary protect their interests by buying the vessel themselves.

Payment of Price

The price must be paid in cash unless a bank guarantee is put up.

Distribution of the Proceeds

Creditors who have claims against the proceeds must file their claims with the creditor who requested the enforced sale and with the Court.

In respect of priority Netherlands law recognises mortgages and maritime liens.

In case of foreign vessels the question whether the claim has a priority depends upon the law governing the claim. As far as the rank of the priority is concerned the lex fori is applicable.

It is possible for the creditors by unanimous agreement to decide as to the distribution between themselves of the proceeds of sale.

Appeal Proceedings

An appeal can be made against the decisions by the Court in respect of the forced sale.

International Conventions

The Netherlands have so far not adhered to the 1967 Brussels Convention on Mortgages on Ships and Maritime Liens and Mortgages on Ships under Construction respectively.

Alex. Rein

Norway

Grounds for an enforced Sale

Section 177 of the Enforcement Act 1915 ('tvangsfullbyrdelsesloven') provides:

'The holder of a lien right ('panterett') in a ship may, after due date, in case of default, seek satisfaction by forced sale by auction . . . or forced operation . . . of the ship, but not in any other manner.

No special basis for enforcement is necessary where satisfaction is sought on the basis of

1. a lien right created by distraint provided that the basis for enforcement has become absolute ('rettskraftig');
2. a lien right created by a registered mortgage instrument or deed of division of estate in probate, provided that the instrument secures a fixed amount, or that the amount of the claim has been determined in a basis for enforcement which has become absolute, or has been admitted in writing;
3. a lien right imposed by law for state or municipal taxes or dues.

In other cases the holder of the lien must obtain judgment or other equivalent basis for enforcement . . . '

'Other equivalent basis' may be an agreement having, by law, the effect of a judgment, arbitral awards in accordance with Norwegian law, etc.

Authority

The 'Namsretten,' a court of the first instance charged with the handling of cases of enforcement.

Care and Maintenance of the Vessel pending Sale

The law has no provisions regarding the preservation of the vessel prior to the sale.

Up to 1st January, 1973, there was a maritime lien for the cost of preserving the ship in the common interest of creditors. This provision has now been deleted as Norway has ratified the 1967 liens and mortgages convention (see Art. 4 of the Convention).

It is not clear whether 'the cost awarded by the court' (art. 11.2 of the Convention) includes costs of preservation, and the same uncertainty exists now in the national law.

Appraisal

No official valuation is made prior to the sale.

Notice of Sale

A notice must be inserted in the official gazette. At least 30 days shall have elapsed between the first publication in the official gazette and the auction.

All holders of registered lien rights (mortgagees, etc.) and all holders of rights who have reported to the court and such holders known to the court shall be notified if they have a known residence or representative. Notification shall be made by registered letter, but no minimum of time from notification to the auction is required.

A notice of the sale is sent to the register of the vessel.

It is further required that particulars as to title to the vessel and mortgages on the vessel and other registered encumbrances on the vessel are obtained from the register of the vessel.

Form of actual Sale

The sale is made by Namsretten at a public auction.

Minimum Price or any Price

The lowest acceptable bid must cover all encumbrances and rights ranking prior to the right of the plaintiff (the person requesting the sale). In this connection maritime liens are taken into account only if confirmed by judgment or if the court consider it clear that they are validly existing.

It is possible for the creditors to be present and if necessary buy the vessel to protect their interests.

Payment of Price

The price is paid to the Court. Cash payment is the main rule but the Court may grant credit in certain cases against security which the Court deems satisfactory.

Distribution of the Proceeds

Creditors having a claim against the proceeds must report to the Court and substantiate their claims.

The ranking of claims is in accordance with the 1967 liens and mortgages Convention. There are no statutory liens other than maritime liens. Right of retention takes precedence over mortgages, but not over maritime liens.

The national law applies equivalently to ships entered in the register of ships of a foreign country.

There is a possibility for the creditors to agree between themselves as to the distribution. However, there are no provisions on this point. Broadly speaking, such an agreement would require the consent of all legally protected interests concerned, including the defendant (debtor) and guarantors.

Appeal Proceedings

The ruling ('kjennelse') confirming the acceptance of a bid may be appealed against (by 'kjaeremål') within two weeks from its making. The same applies to the ruling on the distribution of the proceeds.

The appellate court is the Court of Appeals ('Lagmannsretten'). New appeal to the Supreme Court is allowed in certain cases, but appeal on the grounds that the decision is materially wrong only if the point at issue is the interpretation of a statutory provision.

International Conventions

Norway has ratified the two Brussels Conventions of 1967 in respect of mortgages and liens on vessel and title and mortgages on vessels under construction.

Other Points of Interest

As an alternative to enforced sale by auction the court may grant an application for enforced operation of the ship for the benefit of the mortgagees, by a manager appointed by the court. The manager must fulfil the conditions for owning ships under Norwegian flag.

T.H.A.Potts

Singapore

Grounds for an enforced Sale

A judgment or order from the Court is necessary for an enforced sale of a vessel under arrest in proceedings commenced in the Singapore Court.

In theory it is possible in certain circumstances (for example the Port of Singapore Authority has statutory power to detain and sell vessels of its own motion for payment of port dues etc.) but to proceed without the sanction of an Order of Court is so unusual that the writer has never known of such a case in his experience. Even where such a statutory power as above-mentioned exists, we would certainly advise a client nevertheless to go through the medium of the Courts.

Authority

The sale is handled by the Sheriff.

Care and Maintenance of the Vessel pending Sale

The vessel is in the care of the Sheriff. He will make such arrangements as he considers necessary. If the parties consider that the Sheriff is not doing what ought to be done then they have power to apply to the Court for an order directing the Sheriff to take whatever action the Court considers necessary. The expenses of preservation are met out of the proceeds of sale and enjoy the highest priority.

Appraisal

The appropriate procedure in Singapore provides for the appraisement of the vessel prior to the sale. The appraised figure is communicated in secrecy to the Sheriff prior to the sale taking place. The vessel will not be sold at below the appraised figure at a public auction. If it is desired to sell below the appraised figure then again the Court's permission must be obtained.

Notice of Sale

A public notice must be given usually not less than two weeks prior to the sale.

There is no necessity for a direct notification to a mortgagee but only for general advertisement. Where a vessel is under arrest it is up to mortgagees and other creditors to enforce their rights as rapidly as possible.

Form of actual Sale

The sale is conducted by the auctioneer appointed by the Court on the Sheriff's recommendation. The sale is conducted by public auction. However, it is possible with the Court's approval of the appropriate contract in question (on the Court being satisfied that the price is a good one) for a vessel to be sold by private treaty. A creditor such as a mortgagee who is interested will upon the order for sale being made apply to the Court for leave to bid at the auction and this permission is readily granted.

Minimum Price or any Price

See above under heading 'Appraisal.'

Payment of Price

If the sale is by auction the price is paid in cash into Court. If it is desired to arrange for credit terms this will usually be done by making an application for sale by private treaty when the credit terms will be specified in the contract. Proceeds of sale of a ship in Court provided they exceed the sum of $200,000.00 can by application of an interested party be placed on deposit at interest with the Accountant-General in Singapore pending determination of any question as to priority.

Distribution of the Proceeds

Creditors must all issue Writs in respect of their claims and obtain judgment.

Different claims have different priority ranking. It is not possible to advise in detail on questions of priorities but generally speaking the necessary information can be obtained by a perusal of the relevant section of *McGuffie on Admiralty Practice* which is a book on the English law on this subject which would be regarded as authoritative in Singapore.

A short summary can be made in the following way. The money in Court is distributed to the claimants in the order of the priorities recognised by the Court. In broad terms the order of priorities is, 1. Admiralty Marshal's charges; 2. the costs and expenses of the Plaintiff who effects the arrest and thereby assumes responsibility for the cost of maintaining the vessel under arrest; 3. maritime liens: Master's and crew's wages, collision claims, salvage; 4. a possessory lien; 5. claims of mortgagees; 6. other claims giving rise to a statutory lien.

In case of foreign vessels lex fori is applied.

It is possible for the creditors by unanimous agreement to decide as to the distribution between themselves of the proceeds of sale.

Appeal Proceedings

In respect of any decision of a High Court Judge or an inferior judicial officer and whether it be as the result of a full trial on the substance of a dispute or whether it be in relation to any interlocutory matter, there is always a right of appeal. If the decision complained of is that of a Registrar an appeal lies in first place from his decision to a single Judge. Once the matter has gone before a single Judge there is then a right of appeal to the Court of Appeal which is a tribunal consisting of three Judges none of them, of course, being the Judges who have decided the matter when it came before a single Judge.

Finally if a litigant is still dissatisfied with the decision of the Court of Appeal then subject to certain safeguards for example as to amount in issue and the necessity of furnishing deposits by way of security for costs (in a comparatively nominal amount) a right of appeal lies to the Privy Council in London. Such appeals of course are extremely expensive and should not be undertaken except in matters of great importance in principle or involving very substantial sums of money.

International Conventions

Singapore has not adhered to any International Conventions in respect of maritime liens and mortgages on ships or mortgages on ships under construction.

The Maritime Law Association of the Republic of South Africa

South Africa

Grounds for an enforced Sale

An enforced sale of a vessel does require an Order of Court.

However, there is provision in the Merchant Shipping Act 1951 for the forfeiture of a vessel at the instance of the Director of Merchant Shipping (a Government official) after due notice to all interested parties, including the owner, and in the case of a foreign vessel, to the Consular representative of the country in which the ship is registered. Such notice gives the owner or other interested persons a period of 30 (thirty) days within which to give notice to the Director in writing that he claims the release of the ship, and if release is claimed, provision is made for the interested party to make application to a Court of competent jurisdiction for the release within a stipulated period. If such application is not made timeously or, if, having been made, it is dismissed by the Court, the vessel can be ordered to be forfeited in which case it becomes the property of the State upon the expiry of a further stipulated period (Section 336).

Authority

A sale in execution is handled by the Deputy Sheriff, an official who is appointed by the Department of Justice of the Republic, but who is not a servant of the State.

Care and Maintenance of the Vessel pending Sale

Unless the judgment creditor otherwise directs the Deputy Sheriff takes possession of the ship. It is the Deputy Sheriff's responsibility to see that it is preserved, and any money he may disburse to this end is deducted, along with his remuneration, from the proceeds of the sale. In practice, however, the owner or the creditor or both of them will in all likelihood see to it that it is preserved, as they obviously are both concerned with the protection of their interests.

Appraisal

No official valuation of the vessel is made prior to the sale.

Notice of Sale

Where any movable property (i.e. a ship) is attached the Deputy Sheriff sells it by public auction to the highest bidder after due advertisement by him in two suitable newspapers circulating in the district where the ship is situated and after the expiration of not less than fourteen days from the time of the attachment of the ship. Apart from such advertisement, there is no special provision for the prior notification of a mortgagee, with the result that a foreign mortgagee may not be aware of the proposed sale. The sale would be subject to any real right of a third party but there is some doubt as to whether a mortgage registered in a foreign country confers a right recognised as a real right in the Republic of South Africa (see under heading Distribution of the Proceeds of Sale below).

It is not necessary for particulars as to the title to the vessel and in regard to any mortgages and other registered encumbrances to be obtained from the register of the vessel.

Form of actual Sale

The Deputy Sheriff handles the sale at a public auction.

Minimum Price or any Price

The vessel is sold at the highest price bid, and there is no provision for fixing a reserve or minimum price. Creditors may attend the sale to protect their interests by buying the vessel themselves.

Payment of Price

Payment must be made in cash to the Deputy Sheriff. Although there is no provision for credit, it is possible that in practice a guarantee might be arranged to the satisfaction of the Deputy Sheriff, but this will only be for a very restricted period.

Distribution of the Proceeds

A creditor who wishes to participate in the distribution must give notice to the Deputy Sheriff. This is given by lodging a warrant of execution with him. All warrants so lodged before the date of the sale rank pro rata in the distribution of the proceeds in the order of preference laid down.

Liens are recognised as conferring a preference, and, legal authorities appear to indicate that a lien for essential repairs will have first priority. A mortgage registered at a foreign port would, as the decided cases presently indicate, probably not be recognised as having a preference. The only recorded decided case on this point is a rather old decision in the matter of *In Re Mangoro* (1913 NLR 67) a decision of the full Bench of the Natal Provincial Division to the effect that a foreign mortgagee would not be preferred to local creditors. Recent legal opinion, however, indicates that this decision might be overruled today in a case referred to the appellate Division of the Supreme Court, assuming this were to happen.

It is possible for the creditors to agree as to the distribution of the proceeds provided that they represent all of the creditors who have notice of the proposed sale. There is, however, no specific provision for this.

Appeal Proceedings

If an application were made to the Supreme Court to prevent or set aside the sale, an appeal against the Court's decision would lie to a full Bench (i.e. three Judges) of the provincial division of the Supreme Court concerned. A further appeal against their decision would lie to the Appellate Division of the Supreme Court at Bloemfontein with the leave of the full Bench, or in the event of this being refused, on leave granted upon petition to the Chief Justice of the Appellate Division.

International Conventions

The Republic of South Africa has not signed any Convention relating to enforced sales of vessels.

Other Points of Interest

Our law does not make any special provision for the sale of ships. The ordinary provisions relating to the sale of any movable property in the execution of a judgment pursuant to the Rules of Court would apply. In the case of a ship, the amount involved would invariably be such as to confer jurisdiction in the Supreme Court of South Africa. Consequently, the rules of the Magistrates' Courts, which have jurisdiction on a lower scale, have not been considered here.

In conclusion, it should be noted that the transfer of ownership of vessels when they are sold is subject to the provisions of the Merchant Shipping Act 1951, in so far as the vessel may be registered in the Republic of South Africa.

The Cape and Natal Provincial Divisions of the Supreme Court are also vested with Admiralty jurisdiction and the Rules of Court relating to such Courts make provision for the appraisement and sale of vessels on the order of a judge being obtained in that regard. The relevant section in the Rules is No. 138 which reads as follows –

'The judge may, either before or after final judgment, order any property under the arrest of the Court to be appraised, or to be sold with or without appraisement, and either by public auction or by private contract.'

Ignacio Arroyo

Spain

Grounds for an enforced Sale

In Spain two categories of grounds are required for an enforced sale of vessel: (i) conditions of substance and (ii) conditions of procedure.

The Spanish Code of Commerce allows a judicial sale of a ship in two cases only: (a) for the benefit of maritime creditors; and (b) when the vessel becomes unseaworthy in the course of a voyage. In the first case a judgment from the judge is required. But if the ship is laden and fitted out for a voyage, neither the arrest nor the judgment can be enforced except for debts contracted for the fitting out and provisioning of the vessel for the voyage. Even in that situation the arrest will be lifted if any one concerned in the voyage gives security for the return of the ship within the period fixed by the terms of the security.

The second case is an exception to the general rule by which the Captain has no power to transfer the title to the ship without an express authorisation from his principal, the shipowner. According to that principle the captain must apply to the judge at the port he reaches, if within Spanish jurisdiction, and to the Spanish Consul or Local Authority if abroad; and the Judge, Consul or Local Authority must order a *survey* of the ship. It is also required that if the consignee of the cargo or insurer of the vessel and/or cargo reside or have representatives at the place, they must be summoned to intervene in the proceedings so far as they are concerned. When the damaged condition of the ship and the impossibility of repairing it for the continuation of the voyage have been ascertained, an *order* in the form of *Warrant* or *Decree* from the judge is necessary to enforce the sale of the ship (Arts. 578–579 Code of Commerce).

Authority

Spain has no Admiralty Courts such as England or Courts with specific authority in admiralty matters such as the U.S. The judiciary system in Spain does not reserve to Commercial Courts (i.e. France) the decision in maritime cases. Thus the judge competent in an enforced sale of vessel is the Judge of First Instance, that is to say a single judge of first degree with authority in general matters. The sale is presided over and carried out by the Judge of First Instance at the home port of the ship.

When the vessel is sold for creditors with priority the competent judge is that of the port where the ship is lying (Art. 584 Code of Commerce).

If the ship is abroad and urgent circumstances require the enforcement, the Spanish Consul is the authority to handle the sale according to Article 2110 of the Civil Procedure Act.

Care and Maintenance of the Vessel pending Sale

The absence in Spanish Law of specific provisions on maritime proceedings raise particular problems in connection with this heading. First of all it seems to be clear that depending on the nature of the ship, whether she is a real estate or a chattel, the rules to apply are different. On the other hand according to Article 585 of the Code of Commerce in all legal respects other than those which are modified or restricted by the law laid down by this Code (i.e. mortgages), ships are treated as chattels. However, it is highly controversial whether the general rules on 'administration of chattels under arrest' apply to vessels.

The author feels that the state of the law (statute and case law) on this issue can be summed up as follows:

(i) The vessel is subject to what is called 'judicial administration'.

(ii) As a consequence of that status the ship is in the care of a person proposed by the creditors and appointed by the Judge. The creditor himself can be that person, but the debtor-owner is excluded (vid. Articles 1450 and 1454 of Civil Procedure Act).

(iii) The person in care of the ship is entitled to take whatever action he considers necessary to maintain the vessel. He can in fact also order a new voyage. The freight earned, after deducting the expenses, are added to the proceeds of the sale of the vessel.

(iv) The Judge will send an official document of the order of arrest of the vessel to the Mercantile Register of the place where she is registered. The Registrar must enter the notice of the arrest in the special Book of Ships. The same procedure must be observed when the judgment is issued by the Judge.

Appraisal

Here again general rules apply. Thus the provisions regarding execution call for the appraisement of the ship prior to the sale. Three surveyors, one nominated by each party and the third by the Judge, have to survey and value the ship. In fact Article 579 of the Code of Commerce stipulates that the hull, rigging, engines, stores and such like furniture are appraised, and an inventory shall be drawn up. According to that principle Article 576 of the same Statute provides that a sale of a ship always includes her apparel, furniture and tackle and machinery, if a steam vessel, as are at the time under the control of the vendor. The sale does not include arms, provisions and fuel.

Notice of the Sale

The warrant or decree ordering the sale is posted in the customary places for public notices. An advertisement is inserted in the newspapers of the port in which the proceedings are taken, and in such other papers as the Court may determine. These advertisements will be repeated at intervals of ten days, and particulars of the publication will be stated in the sales proceedings.

The vendor must deliver to the purchaser a certified copy of the entry of the ship in the Register up to the date of the sale.

Form of actual Sale

The sale is conducted by public auction under the direction of the Judge of First Instance. The sale will take place on the day fixed, and the time for the sale cannot be less than twenty days after notice has been given.

In respect of the place where the sale is performed there is in Spanish Law a difference between the creditors with priority ranking – whose claims will be set out under the heading 'Distribution of the proceeds of sale' – and the ordinary creditors. In the first case ships can be seized and sold judicially in the port in which they are found, at the instance of any of those creditors. In the latter case the ship can only be arrested and sold in its home port (Article 584 of the Code of Commerce).

The form of the actual sale is that prescribed by ordinary Law for Judicial sales. The sale is by auction. The vessel is obtained by the person who gives the highest bid. Each bidder ceases to be bound by his offer when the latter is surpassed by another valid offer. For an offer to be valid the bidder has to deposit 10% of the minimum price.

Minimum Price or any Price obtainable

The minimum price depends on the number of the sessions during which the sale by auction takes place. Thus on the first session the minimum price is the price ascertained by the experts (see above under the heading Appraisal). However, should a bidder offer two thirds of the appraised figure he will get the vessel.

On the second session the minimum price will be 80% of the appraised value. If not sold at that price another attempt will be made at a new hearing the price being reduced by a further 20%. Further sessions can be held with corresponding reductions of price. Should in spite of these reductions the vessel not be sold the Judge after having heard the creditors concerned and the owners can issue an order to proceed with the sale of the vessel without auction the Judge determining the conditions of such a sale.

Payment of Price

Within eight days from the sale, the buyer must pay the balance in cash. The money is deposited with the Court at creditor's disposal. Debt, interests and litigation fees shall be paid out of this sum. If there is a balance it shall be placed at deposit with the General Bail Account.

After the payment the Judge will serve the debtor an order to deliver the document of transfer of the property of the vessel. From this moment all liabilities of a ship to previous creditors are deemed to be extinguished by a document showing a Judicial sale by public auction, assented to and inscribed in the Mercantile Register.

Distribution of the Proceeds of Sale

In every judicial sale of ship for the benefit of creditors, the debts will be ranked in the following order (Articles 580, 581 of the Code of Commerce).

1. Debts due to the Public Exchequer, which are proved by means of an official certificate from the proper authority.
2. The Court fees for the proceedings.
3. Pilotage and tonnage dues, as well as light and harbour dues.

4. The cost of watching, warehousing and preservation from the time of entry of the ship into the last port.
5. Claims arising out of the contract of engagement of the master and crew for the last voyage.
6. The repayment of any portion of the cargo which the captain has sold to repair the ship, provided always that the sale is shown to have been by order of Judicial warrant and noted on the ship's register.
7. Debts owing for materials and work and labour in the building of the ship if she has not been to sea, and those necessary for the preservation or the continuation of the voyage (i.e. repairing, fitting, provisions, fuel). Price of the vessel remaining due to the last vendor. The debts enumerated under this heading must, in order to take advantage of this preference, be proved by a contract entered in the Mercantile Register.
8. Unpaid insurance premiums for the last two years pursuant to the hull policy.
9. Indemnity due to the shippers for the value of the goods shipped and not delivered to the consignees, or for damages sustained by them for which the ship is liable.

If the proceeds of sale are insufficient to pay all creditors included in the same class, such proceeds will be divided among them pro rata. In the case that a mortgage is registered against the vessel the ranking of the priorities will be different and more complex. Articles 31–34 of the Ship Mortgage Act 1893, must here be taken into account. Should the proceeds of the sale be sufficient to cover the claims of all creditors who have a priority no particular problems will arise. Any balance must be deposited in the General Bail Office for the disposal of ordinary creditors.

The Ship Mortgage Act makes a distinction between those claims which have a priority over a registered mortgage without being registered or noted in the Commercial Register such as taxes, court fees, pilotage, tonnage dues, light and harbour dues, preservation of a vessel, wages to master and crew and insurance premiums and claims which require registration in order to rank above registered mortgages such as bottomry loans, general average contributions, repair costs etc.

Appeal Proceedings

Appeal proceedings are possible. An appeal can be made by either party. Appeal lies to the Court of Appeal ('Audiencia Provincial'). Appeal from the Court of Appeal to the Supreme Court is allowed in certain enumerated circumstances ('recurso de casación').

In the last instance appeal on the grounds that the decision of the inferior Court is materially wrong is allowed only when the point at issue is the misinterpretation of either a statutory provision or a precedent based on a Supreme Court opinion ('doctrina legal').

It is doubtful whether the mere fact of filing an appeal causes the effect of delay of the execution of the sale. The prevailing view gives an affirmative answer. At any rate it should be underlined that the enforcement will be postponed if the claimant furnishes security to cover damages awarded the owner of the vessel in case the enforced sale turns out to be wrongful.

International Conventions

Spain ratified on 2nd June, 1930, the International Convention for the Unification of Certain Rules of Law relating to Maritime Liens and Mortgages, signed at Brussels, April 10, 1926. Further Spain was one of the signatories of the International Convention respecting Arrest of Seagoing Ships, done at Brussels on May 10, 1952. Spain ratified this Convention on September 11, 1953, and some years later passed the 'Arrest of Vessels Act 1967'.

Robert Romlöv

Sweden

Grounds for an enforced Sale

An enforced sale is usually made pursuant to a judgment of the Court against the owner of the vessel.

However, if the owner is declared bankrupt the Receiver, mortgagees and certain preferred creditors, particularly those with maritime liens may apply for an order for sale without first obtaining a judgment.

Authority

The sale is handled by the 'Överexekutor', the regional executory authority, of which there are twenty-three in Sweden.

Care and Maintenance of Vessel pending Sale

On the basis of the judgment the vessel is attached by a local authority (utmätningsman) as a preliminary step to the sale. The vessel is preserved by this local authority, normally in consultation with the applicant, who will have to advance the money necessary for maintenance. The vessel will only be insured at the request of the applicant who then has to advance the premium.

After the sale the said costs will be paid as a first charge on the proceeds.

The sale of a vessel will take place within four months after she has been attached unless the applicant agrees to extend the time.

Appraisal

The local authority effecting the attachement makes a valuation – normally with expert help.

Notice of Sale

a. Notice of the sale primarily directed at potential buyers – normally in the official gazette and in local newspapers – must be published 'in ample time' before the sale. This is normally 3–4 weeks. In special cases – large vessels and foreign vessels – a notice may also be published in International Trade Journals.
b. Notice to the applicant, to the shipowner and to all known creditors holding mortgages, liens etc. must be sent by airmail at least 30 days before the sale.
c. Whether the vessel is Swedish or foreign-owned the Shipping Register is notified of attachment and enforced sales.

Form of actual Sale

The sale will be conducted by an officer of the 'Överexekutor'.

An enforced sale is at public auction, where anybody is entitled to participate and bid for the vessel.

An extract of the Shipping Register showing title, encumbrances, mortgage holders etc. will be obtained by the executory authorities.

Minimum Price or any Price

A minimum price is fixed, being the costs of maintenance and sale of the vessel plus all claims with higher preference than the claim of the applicant. A bid which does not cover the minimum price cannot be accepted, unless all parties concerned agree to it. A creditor with a higher preference than the applicant may join the applicant, thereby reducing the minimum price to cover only claims with higher preference than the party joining the applicant.

Without the consent of the applicant (or the creditor joining the applicant) a bid cannot be accepted which does not cover his claim in full.

Payment of Price

a. In principle 1/6 of the price (or the cost of the sale, if it amounts to more than 1/6) must be paid in cash promptly at the auction and 5/6 not later than when the proceeds are distributed (see answer below).

Instead of a cash payment of the first 1/6, first class security (including mortgage security in the vessel sold) may be accepted by the auctioneer for the time being until distribution of proceeds.

Mortgage holders covered by the bid may agree to allowing their mortgages on the vessel to remain in force instead of taking cash payment, in which case the buyer will also be personally liable for the mortgage.

b. The price must be paid to the 'Överexekutor'.

Distribution of the Proceeds

The proceeds are distributed at a creditors' meeting which will be held at a date fixed by the authority and published in the notice of the sale.

Claims for payment out of the proceeds must be made to the 'Överexekutor' before or at the sale. Claims lodged later will only be met from proceeds not claimed by other creditors.

The priority between different claims are shortly as follows starting with the highest preferred claims:

1. Costs for preservation and sale
2. Maritime liens under the 1967 Convention article 4 : 1
3. Builders' and repairers' possessory liens
4. Ships mortgages
5. The claim secured by the arrest of the vessel.

Between 4 and 5, general preference for wages (to shore personnel), taxes etc. may be granted.

Lex fori and the 1967 Convention are applied in the first place. Priorities not known to Swedish law or to the Convention will be treated according to the law of the country where the vessel is registered but they will rank after Convention priorities.

Disputes between the creditors regarding the distribution of proceeds may be settled by agreement between themselves. A creditor may further reduce his claim or waive his preferential rights. It is, however, unlikely that creditors may otherwise vary the legal provisions e.g. by granting one creditor clearly more than what is properly due to him.

Failing agreement between the creditors the 'Överexekutor' decides questions as to the distribution of proceeds.

Appeal Proceedings

An appeal may be made against the order of sale and/or against the distribution of proceeds. Even if there is an appeal the buyer must pay the price and he may take possession of the vessel after full payment, unless the Court of Appeal orders a stay. If such an order of stay prevents the buyer from taking possession for more than three months, he may rescind the purchase and get his money back.

International Conventions

Sweden denounced the 1926 Convention on Maritime Liens and Mortgages on 1st March, 1965, but ratified the 1967 Convention on 13th November, 1975.

Other Points of Interest

Non-registered vessels, i.e. vessels of less than 12 $\times$ 4 metres and shares in registered vessels are sold under the simpler rules applicable to common movables, requiring less publicity. Registered ships under construction are treated in the same manner as completed ships.

J. G. R. Griggs

United Kingdom

Grounds for an enforced Sale

An order by the Court for the appraisement and sale of the vessel is always necessary. Such an Order will be made after judgment if the vessel is still under arrest. An order may be made pendente lite on the Plaintiff's application in certain circumstances for example where the vessel is deteriorating or where the cost of maintaining the vessel under arrest is disproportionate to its value. The proceeds of sale will then be paid into Court to meet any judgment.

Authority

The sale is handled by the Admiralty Marshal in whose custody the vessel remains until released or sold. The party arresting undertakes to be responsible for the cost of maintaining the vessel under arrest. If the Plaintiff succeeds he will be entitled to recover the cost of arrest from the security, if provided, or from the proceeds of sale if the vessel is sold.

The Marshal is not responsible for insuring the vessel whilst under arrest this being for the parties who have claims against her each for his own interest.

Appraisal

An official appraisal of the value of the vessel is made upon the Order of the Court.

Notice of Sale

Generally on making an Order for the sale of the vessel the Court will require the Admiralty Marshal to sell by public auction or by private treaty for which purpose brokers will be employed and they will be likely to advertise the vessel as in the case of any other sale.

Other creditors including mortgagees will not be notified of the proposed sale but the proceeds of sale will be paid into Court. Thereafter the Court will order the publication of a notice in *Lloyd's List* and other newspapers of the sale requiring claimants against the proceeds to bring their claims to Court within a specified time. The Court after the expiration of the period in question will determine priorities among the different claimants and will distribute the money in Court accordingly.

Form of actual Sale

As mentioned above the Admiralty Marshal sells the vessel by public auction or by private treaty.

The money in Court is distributed to the claimants in the order of the priorities recognised by the Court. In broad terms the order of priorities is, 1. Admiralty Marshal's charges, 2. the costs and expenses of the Plaintiff who effects the arrest and thereby assumes responsibility for the cost of maintaining the vessel under arrest. 3. Maritime liens: Master's and crew's wages, collision claims, salvage. 4. A possessory lien. 5. Claims of mortgagees. 6. Other claims giving rise to a statutory lien.

Minimum Price or any Price

The minimum price will be fixed by the appraisement obtained by the Admiralty Marshal although the vessel may be sold for less by leave of the Court.

Any creditors may bid for the vessel either privately or at an auction.

Payment of Price

The net proceeds of sale must be paid in cash into Court to create the fund in Court for the benefit of the Plaintiff and other creditors.

Distribution of the Proceeds

In order to have an effective claim against the fund in Court the creditor must obtain a judgment of the Court for the amount of his claim.

In Respect of foreign Vessels

The lex fori will be applied although the Court when dealing with a claim involving rights governed by a foreign law will determine the nature of that right by reference to the foreign law. It is possible for all the creditors by unanimous agreement to decide how the fund in Court should be distributed between them.

Appeal Proceedings

Claims against the fund will be dealt with initially by the Admiralty Registrar. From his decision an appeal lies to the Admiralty Judge. From the Judge's decision there is an appeal to the Court of Appeal and from the Court of Appeal with leave to the House of Lords.

International Conventions

The United Kingdom has not yet adhered to the 1967 Brussels Convention on Mortgages on Ships and Maritime Liens nor to the 1967 Brussels Convention on Ships under Construction but is expected to do so in the near future.

John C. McHose

United States of America

Grounds for an enforced Sale

An order of court is necessary for enforced sale.

If any party to an action makes a showing that the property seized is perishable or liable to deterioration or loss of value, or if the expense of keeping it is excessive or disproportionate, or if there is unreasonable delay in securing the release of the property the court may order a sale.

Authority

The sale is handled by the United States Marshal for the District where the seizure is made.

Care and Maintenance of the Vessel pending Sale

The Marshal takes care of the vessel. The Plaintiff who brings the action must pay the Marshal's expenses. A deposit is required and the Marshal usually wants insurance protection provided.

Appraisal

No formal appraisal is made prior to sale. The parties will probably have their own appraisals made.

Notice of Sale

Notice is published and six days is the usual minimum time, although the court could order a shorter time.

Notice is usually given to a mortgagee if known.

Notice is not sent to the Register of the vessel.

It is not required that particulars as to title to the vessel and mortgages on the vessel and other registered encumbrances on the vessel are obtained from the Register of the vessel.

Form of actual Sale

The United States Marshal handles the sale by public auction.

Minimum Price or any Price

The court can in its order for sale attach conditions with respect to price or other requirements.

Creditors can be present and if necessary protect their interests by buying the vessel.

Payment of Price

The sale is usually for cash, although credit might be arranged with court approval.

The price is paid in to the registry of the court.

Distribution of the Proceeds

Creditors lodge their claims in the court action under which the vessel was sold. The court orders the distribution.

Priorities are established by statute and by long established principles of maritime lien priorities.

With respect to priorities a full textbook could be written on the subject. Some guiding lines may be of interest.

Basically, maritime liens enforceable by suit in rem are the subject of Federal statutes (46 USC Sections 971 through 975). However, the statutes do not define priorities. Section 974 provides that nothing in the statutes shall be construed to affect the rules of law existing on June 5, 1920, in regard to (1) the right to proceed against the vessel for advances, (2) laches in the enforcement of liens upon vessels, (3) the right to proceed in personam, (4) the rank of preferred maritime liens among themselves, or (5) priorities between maritime liens and mortgages, other than preferred mortgages, upon vessels of the United States.

There are also statutes in most states which pertain to maritime liens, and in many cases the courts will look to such statutes in determining priorities.

In addition, there are court rules in some Federal districts which state local rules with respect to maritime liens.

There is some authority to the effect that priority of liens will be governed by the lex fori.

There are a number of cases which hold in effect that generally by the weight of authority maritime liens, irrespective of the time of their creation, have the following order of priority:

(1) seamen's wages;
(2) salvage;
(3) tort and collision liens;
(4) repairs, supplies, towage, wharfage, pilotage and other necessaries;
(5) bottomry bonds in inverse order of application; and
(6) non-maritime liens.

There is also authority that in the case of vessels engaged in commerce on the ocean, the voyage rule applies, i.e., liens for necessaries furnished on the last voyage rank liens for prior voyages.

In the case of vessels engaged in commerce on the Great Lakes and waterways not usable in winter, the 'season rule' usually applies.

In the case of 'harbour vessels' on the Atlantic Coast, claims less than forty days old rank older ones. However, in Washington state a period of ninety days is specified by a local court rule.

There is also case authority holding that marshalling liens of equal rank depends on conditions and circumstances with respect to the respective liens.

46 USC 975 provides: 'This chapter shall supersede the provisions of all State statutes conferring liens on vessels, insofar as such statutes purport to create rights of action to be enforced by suits in rem in admiralty against vessels for repairs, supplies, towage, use of dry dock or marine railway, and other necessaries.'

There are many cases which hold that claims which are liens under the general maritime law have priority over claims of mortgages, regardless whether the mortgages were registered before or after such liens accrued.

There are some jurisdictions in which liens other than those listed above are fixed by law, e.g., insurance premiums may be liens with priority over a preferred ship mortgage. A lien for unpaid premiums on insurance on a vessel, whether maritime or statutory, has been held to be subordinate to liens for supplies and repairs.

There is authority that advances to a shipowner on the vessel's credit, out of which maritime claims are paid, entitles the person making the advances to a maritime lien of equal rank with similar claims.

There is authority holding that a maritime lien has precedence over the right of forfeiture in condemnation proceedings.

There is also a substantial body of law involving laches on the part of maritime lienors. The general rule is that laches must be decided on general principles of equity and fair dealing.

In respect of foreign vessels lex fori will apply.

It is possible for the creditors by unanimous agreement to decide as to the distribution between themselves of the proceeds of sale.

Appeal Proceedings

It is possible to appeal from decisions by the Trial Court.

International Conventions

The United States have not ratified an international Convention affecting enforced sales of vessels.

GPSR Compliance

The European Union's (EU) General Product Safety Regulation (GPSR) is a set of rules that requires consumer products to be safe and our obligations to ensure this.

If you have any concerns about our products, you can contact us on ProductSafety@springernature.com

In case Publisher is established outside the EU, the EU authorized representative is:

Springer Nature Customer Service Center GmbH
Europaplatz 3
69115 Heidelberg, Germany

Batch number: 10830943

Printed by Printforce, the Netherlands